UNNECESSARY WARS?

UNNECESSARY WARS?

CAUSES AND EFFECTS OF UNITED STATES WARS

FROM THE AMERICAN REVOLUTION TO VIETNAM

by

Peter M. Rinaldo

DorPete Press   Briarcliff Manor, New York

Library of Congress Catalog
Card Number 93-070883

Grateful acknowledgement is made to Stanley Karnow for permission to use the map of Viet Nam in Chapter IV, originally published in *Vietnam: A History*, Copyright © 1984 by Stanley Karnow, and to
Paul Kennedy for permission to use the map of Europe in Chapter VII, originally published in *The Rise and Fall of the Great Powers*, Copyright © 1987 by Paul Kennedy, reprinted by permission of Random House, Inc.

Publisher's Cataloging in Publication
(Prepared by Quality Books Inc.)

Rinaldo, Peter M. (Peter Merritt), 1922-
　　Unnecessary wars? : causes and effects of United States wars from the American Revolution to Vietnam / by Peter M. Rinaldo.
　　p. cm.
　　Preassigned LCCN: 93-070883.
　　ISBN 0-9622123-7-7

　　1. United States--History, Military.　I. Title.

E181.R56 1993　　　　　　　973
　　　　　　　　　　　　　　　QBI93-658

Contents

Chapter I

INTRODUCTION

Hawks, Doves, and the National Interest

B etween the Declaration of Independence in 1776 and the Bicentennial in 1976, the United States fought eight major wars: the American Revolution, the War of 1812, the Civil War, the Spanish-American War, World War I, World War II, the Korean War, and the Vietnam War. There were also a number of minor wars and skirmishes, such as the Mexican-American War. This book examines the causes and results of the eight major wars and tries to assess the degree to which they were necessary, as well as reviews some potential conflicts that did not occur.

The concept of necessity can have different meanings. Once an event has passed, it can be said to have had an historical necessity simply because it occurred, as in the dictionary definition of *necessary* as "determined or produced by the previous condition of things." However, the word can also refer to whether an event was "absolutely needed." It is this latter sense that is used in this book.

Inevitably, this involves playing games of "What if?"; in particular, what would have been the historical outcome if the war had not taken place. Could the goals that led to the declaration of war have been accomplished without armed conflict? In the cases of the three wars included in

UNNECESSARY WARS?

the section Probably Unnecessary Wars — the War of 1812, the Spanish-American War, and the Vietnam War — there is sufficient historical evidence to indicate that conflict probably could have been avoided.

In the cases of the American Revolution and the American Civil War, though, it is much more difficult to see how they could have been avoided, given the personalities and historical forces involved. Still, I have classified these wars as Possibly Unnecessary Wars. In making this judgement, I have used the scientific concept of a "controlled experiment." Unfortunately, history is not an exact science. In physics or chemistry, the scientist can conduct a controlled experiment in which two tests are run, one maintaining a base set of conditions and one in which one of the conditions is changed. In medicine, one patient is treated with a new drug while the control receives a placebo. In history, the closest one can come to a controlled experiment is to find two different countries with some similarities and observe the difference produced if one goes to war and the other does not. Since no two countries are ever exactly similar, the comparison is inexact but can yield some insight into the validity of the assumption that there was a possibility, albeit remote, that these wars also might have been unnecessary.

The next section considers the two World Wars and the Korean War. Although theoretically an isolationist United States could have avoided participation in these wars, in practice I believe that our participation was both just and necessary. However, I also believe that there is a legitimate question as to whether these wars were necessary for the national interest of the powers that initiated the conflicts, and I have grouped these wars in a section called Wars Unnecessary for the Aggressor. Thus, these chapters will explore the history of the diplomatic negotiations prior to the onset of these wars, as well as the incidents that directly led to American involvement.

Introduction

The following chapter examines three potential wars that were avoided — "Fifty-Four-Forty or Fight!", the Venezuelan Border Dispute, and the Cuban Missile Crisis. One might say that the wars which were averted were *obviously unnecessary* since they did not have to occur to resolve the matters in dispute. Thus, along with *probably unnecessary*, *possibly unnecessary*, and *unnecessary for the aggressor*, *obviously unnecessary* completes the classification of the four types of unnecessary wars.

Throughout the book, I have omitted any account of the battles that took place during the wars under consideration. The events leading up to the war and the war aims are analyzed, as are the results of the peace treaty, but the war itself is treated as a "black box." What happened during a war has little or no relationship to the question of whether the war was necessary or not, and so these details are not germane to this book.

In determining whether a war was necessary or not, I have used the following criteria for an <u>unnecessary</u> war:
A. It failed to achieve any of the aims that led to the declaration of war, OR IF
B. the war did achieve its aims initially, but these proved to be short-lived, OR IF
C. the aims could have been achieved without resort to war.

The question of necessity is examined separately from the question of justice. (A good discussion of "just wars" can be found in Michael Walzer's 1977 book *Just and Unjust Wars*.) A war can be a just war but still unnecessary according to the above criteria. However, I do not believe the converse is possible; that is, that an unjust war could ever be necessary.[1]

Further, a war may have been unnecessary but still may have had a profound influence on subsequent history. With the exception of the potential wars reviewed in Chapter

UNNECESSARY WARS?

X, all of the wars examined in this book actually took place, with consequences different from those that would have resulted from a similar period of peace. In some cases, these consequences were very favorable. For instance, most wars stimulated the economy. However, this sort of consequence is in the nature of a side effect. No rational person would propose starting a war simply because it would lead to favorable economic trends.

The subtitle of this introductory chapter is Hawks, Doves, and the National Interest. According to the historian of American usage William Safire, the term "war hawk" was a coinage of Thomas Jefferson's in 1798 to describe those in the opposition Federalist party who wished to start a war with France. "War hawks" later was used by the Jeffersonian Republican John Randolph to designate those in his party, such as Henry Clay and John Calhoun, who wanted to go to war against Great Britain. The antonym of the hawk, the dove, has been a symbol of peace since the time of the ancient Greeks, whose love goddess Aphrodite was often depicted with a dove on her arm. More recently. the painter Pablo Picasso's depiction of a dove was used by the Communists as a peace symbol in their posters. In current usage, doves favor negotiation and accommodation to achieve our nation's foreign policy goals, whereas hawks favor the use of force to obtain our aims.[2]

Throughout history, individuals fitting the categories of hawk and dove have influenced their country's policies. The Greek historian Thucydides tells of the debate between Nicias and Alcabiades about instigating a war against Sicily after the death of the great statesman Pericles. Nicias, an aristocrat, in this instance espoused the doveish viewpoint; his rival, Alcabiades, advocated an imperialism that eventually led to war.[3] Generally, in the United States, the hawks have predominated. A hawkish individual is usually seen as selfless, with the goal only of safeguarding the interests of the nation. In theory, the hawk is willing to make the ultimate sacrifice of dying for his nation, although in practice this sacrifice is usually made by others. The dove, on the other hand, is often seen as having an ulterior motive for pacifism. In the past, most merchants have been doves, since wars disrupt international trade, which has led to charges of their putting personal interest above national interest. Also, doves often question whether it is really worthwhile to die for the cause being advocated by the hawks, and thus are perceived as being wimpish or cowardly. Moreover, the dove has often been perceived as being unpatriotic. However, in political terms, it is often unclear as to whether or not the hawks hold the moral high ground. Until the First World War, the majority of the U.S. populace usually tended to be bellicose. Politicians could secure reelection by taking a hawkish line. On the other hand, those politicians who took the dovish view that the use of force in a particular instance was not justified found themselves with a minority of votes as the result of taking what they regarded as a principled stand. Because the debates between the hawks and the doves have been important in the decision to go to war in each of the conflicts considered in this book, the chapters include biographical sketches of some of the principal hawks and doves in each period.

Any assessment of whether a war was necessary or not must consider the question of national interest. The leaders who took us into each of these conflicts undoubtedly convinced themselves that it was in the national interest to do so. As long as we live in a world of nation states, the national governments are expected to maximize the long-term welfare of their nations, even if their actions are detrimental to the welfare of other nations. The difficulty comes in trying to assess the relative importance of the positive and negative results that war will bring. Is the asset of territorial gain worth the liability of deaths of hundreds or thousands of soldiers? Is it worth spending national treasures of money and manpower to avenge an insult to the national honor? In

UNNECESSARY WARS?

the process of analyzing the question of whether a war was necessary or not, we shall try to conclude whether the war really was in the national interest.

Finally, although the Constitution vests the power to declare war in Congress, its vote is usually in response to a message from the President advocating such action. Thus, the character of the President inevitably is an important factor in whether or not the nation goes to war. A strong President can resist the pressure of the war hawks to enter an unnecessary war, whereas a weak one will be unable to stand up to them. The reader will find examples of both the strong and the weak in the pages that follow.

Hundreds, and in some cases thousands, of books have been written about each of the wars considered in this volume. During my research, I could not possibly read them all, but I satisfied myself that in each case there existed an agreed set of historical facts. However, I also found that there was wide disagreement among the various historians on interpretation of these facts, such as in determining the principal cause of a war. Thus, since professional historians have disagreed so markedly in the past on historical interpretation of the causes and effects of wars, I feel less hesitant in offering my own interpretation in this book. If nothing else, my views should stir up the historians who disagree!

PROBABLY

UNNECESSARY

WARS

Chapter II

THE WAR OF 1812

The developments leading up to the first two wars examined in this section of the book, the War of 1812 and the Spanish-American War, followed a similar pattern. There were provocative acts by an adversary. These were reported in the press and led to popular indignation. In both wars, there also were undercurrents of territorial expansionism. Some politicians, reflecting both the feelings of their constituents and their own expansionist agenda, pressed the Administration to take action. In both cases, the Administration was led by weak Presidents—in one case James Madison and in the other, William McKinley. Both men felt that they had to accede to the wishes of the martial wings of their political parties. Even though the adversary at the last minute agreed to cease the offensive conduct that led to demands for war in the first place, the decision to go to war was maintained.

HISTORICAL BACKGROUND OF THE WAR OF 1812

The early years of the nineteenth century were momentous ones in Europe. In 1804 Napoleon secured a popular vote sanctioning his title of Emperor of the French. He commenced a series of successful military campaigns, and by 1807 he dominated all of Europe except Great Britain, Russia, and Sweden. In that year he met with Czar Alexander I of Russia, and they agreed, in a treaty signed on board a raft in the Niemen River, to divide Europe between their two empires. Napoleon proposed a "Continental system" that would close Europe to British trade and force that "nation of shopkeepers," as he contemptuously called Britain, to sue for peace. Not all of Europe remained willingly under Napoleon. The Spanish revolted in 1808 and were aided by the British in what was known as the Peninsular War. Russia soon deserted the Continental system, and Napoleon marched on Moscow, which he reached in September of 1812.

Although most American historians have tended to downplay the relationship between the Napoleonic Wars and the contemporaneous events in North America, Canadian historians, in particular, have tended to see the United States as involved during the War of 1812 in an undeclared alliance with the French. The Canadian historian Egerton Ryerson wrote in 1880:

> At the darkest hour of that eventful contest, when the continent of Europe was drenched with the blood of nations, the Tyrant had his feet upon their neck, and England alone stood erect, taxing her resources to the utmost and shedding her best blood for human freedom, the Democratic party in the United States -- the ever anti-British party -- the pro-slavery party -- the party in the United States least subordinate to law and most inimical to liberty.....declared war against Britain and forthwith invaded Canada.[1]

Sidney F. Wise, who included the above quotation in his article "The War of 1812 in Popular History," commented further that in the view of Canadian historians, "Canadians, therefore, were essentially victims, caught up by their colonial status in the titanic struggle being waged in Europe and by their proximity to a revolutionary state now waxing in power and rapaciousness."[2] American historians, in general, have not shared these views.

The direct effect of the Napoleonic Wars on the United States was on its overseas trade. In his Continental system instituted by decree in 1807, Napoleon declared the Continent closed to British goods and ordered the seizure of any neutral vessel that had touched at a British port. Britain responded with Orders in Council, which forbade neutral vessels to trade with any countries under Napoleon's control unless such vessels had touched at a British port. Thus, France seized all neutral vessels that touched at British ports, and Britain seized those that did not do so.

Under the initiative of President Thomas Jefferson, Congress on December 22, 1807, passed a law forbidding U.S. ships to leave American harbors for foreign ports. This effectively prevented the seizure of the ships, but it also was financially disastrous for merchants engaged in overseas trade. New England merchants alone lost $8 million in fifteen months following passage of the law.[3] Consequently, under pressure from these mercantile interests, Congress repealed the 1807 act on March 1, 1809 and in its stead passed a Nonintercourse Act with Britain and France. A year later this act was repealed and replaced with a bill providing that as soon2 as either Britain or France withdrew its regulations against U.S. shipping, the Nonintercourse Act would be revived against the other country. Napoleon grabbed this opening to announce that French decrees against U.S. shipping were repealed. John Quincy Adams, then minister to Russia, warned that this announcement was "a trap to catch us into a war with England," but President James Madison, who had succeeded Jefferson, did not listen. Madison gave an ultimatum to Britain to withdraw its Orders in Council; Britain stood fast, and again Congress forbade all trade with Britain and its colonies. Although France continued to seize and scuttle American vessels, President Madison insisted that "The national faith was pledged to France."[4]

BRITISH ACTS INFLAMING AMERICAN PUBLIC OPINION

British actions adversely aroused American public opinion in three different areas:

Harassment of American Naval and Merchant Ships

On June 22, 1807, the British ship *Leopard* opened fire on the American frigate *Chesapeake* off the coast of Virginia because the American ship refused to stop to be searched for British deserters. Three of the *Chesapeake*'s crew were killed and eighteen wounded. There was considerable public pressure to declare war against Britain for violating U.S. sovereignty. However, instead, President Jefferson stood up to the hawkish demands and decided to resort to "peaceful coercion." He requested Congress to pass the Embargo Act of 1807, mentioned above, which it did.

After this act was repealed in 1809, there were further incidents. In 1811 the American frigate *President* was fired upon by the British sloop of war *Little Belt*. This time the American ship won the engagement, but public opinion was again outraged.

Impressment of American Seamen

In the early nineteenth century, Great Britain had a system of selective service for its military forces that was known as impressment. Groups of able-bodied men were rounded up against their will and impressed into His Majesty's service. Aside from the somewhat arbitrary and capricious nature of selection, this "draft" was no different in principle from that imposed from time to time by many countries, including the United States. However, British seamen so inducted did not like it, and when they had the opportunity, they deserted to American vessels, which provided higher wages, better food, and better treatment.

During this period of the Napoleonic Wars, Great Britain maintained that it had the right to search merchant vessels of neutral countries, including the United States, for contraband of war. As the British historian William James stated, "If, in the exercise of that right, the belligerent should discover on board the neutral vessel a subject who has withdrawn himself from his lawful allegiance, the neutral can have no fair ground for refusing to deliver him up; more especially if that subject is proved to be a deserter from the sea or land service of the former."[5]

The problem was that it was very difficult to distinguish between recent deserters, former deserters who had become naturalized American citizens, and other American citizens who had emigrated years before but still had British accents. Theodore Roosevelt, the American President who was also an historian, states in his history *The Naval War of 1812*:

> Any innocent merchant vessel was liable to seizure at any moment; and when overhauled by a British cruiser short of men was sure to be stripped of most of her crew. The British officers themselves were the judges as to whether a seaman should be pronounced a native of America or of Britain, and there was no appeal from their judgment. If a captain lacked his full complement, there was little doubt as to the view he would take of any man's nationality. The wrongs inflicted on our seafaring countrymen by their impressment into foreign ships formed the main cause of the war.[6]

Bradford Perkins in his book *Prologue to War* examines the impressment question in detail. He estimates that during the ten years prior to the War of 1812, about half of the total seamen serving on American ships engaged in foreign trade were British sailors. numbering about 9,000 men. Although some of these became naturalized U.S. citizens, the British generally did not recognize that naturalization relieved British-born sailors of their duty to serve the Crown. Perkins concludes that during this period, in addition to British sailors repatriated, at least 3,800 American seamen were impressed, with the number possibly as high as 6,500. As a result of complaints filed with Britain, about 2,000 American seamen were released before the war and 1,800 more after the war.[7]

Presumed British/Canadian Support for the Indians

In the twenty years following the American Revolution, pioneers continued to push their settlements into the South and the West, which inevitably brought them in conflict with the Indians. The historian Samuel Eliot Morison states, "Although the Indians faithfully fulfilled their treaty stipulations, white pioneers in the Northwest committed the most wanton and cruel murders of them, for which it was almost impossible to obtain a conviction from a pioneer jury. From time to time, a few hungry and desperate chiefs were rounded up by government officials and plied with oratory and whisky until they signed a treaty alienating the hunting grounds of their tribe.....Between 1795 and 1809 the Indians parted with some 48 million acres."[8]

Naturally, the Indians resisted. Under the leadership of the Shawnee chief Tecumseh and his medicine-man brother, Tenskwatawa, the Indians formed a league to resist further encroachment on their lands, establishing their headquarters in the Indiana Territory at the point where Tippecanoe Creek joins the Wabash River. This Indian league secured some of its rifles from the British troops in Canada. At a time when Tecumseh was absent, the governor of the territory, William Henry Harrison, marched to the Indian headquarters. There is some question as to whether Harrison really won the

Battle of Tippecanoe on November 7, 1811, since large numbers died on both sides, but Harrison brought his remaining men back to safety and claimed victory, laying the foundation for his election as President in 1840. Further, the presence of British weapons on the Indian side confirmed the American belief that Britain was behind Tecumseh's confederacy.[9]

OTHER FACTORS LEADING TO PRESSURE FOR WAR

The desire by settlers for Indian land was coupled with a desire for land in Canada. Many pioneers simply emigrated to Canada. The Canadian historian Ernest Cruikshank states that by 1810, "One-third of the inhabitants were recent settlers from the United States, who had removed to escape taxation or avoid military service.... John Melish declared his conviction from enquiries made during his visit in 1810 'that if 5,000 men were sent into Upper Canada with a proclamation of independence, the great mass of the people would join the American government.'" [10]

In addition to those Americans who wished to emigrate, there were those who wanted their country to expand. Charles and Mary Beard state in *The Rise of American Civilization*, "All along the frontier from Vermont to Kentucky, advancing pioneers were ready for a new onward surge. Western New York and the Ohio country were filling up with settlers and the call for more virgin soil was being heard in the land."[11]

The Indian question and the expansionist push to Canada were interrelated. After the Battle of Tippecanoe, Tecumseh went to Canada and was welcomed by the governor general, Sir George Prevost. Thus, a conquest of Canada would not only secure more land but also eliminate the base for Indian attacks. A bonus would be to take over the rich fur trade that the Canadians enjoyed with the Indians.

PROBABLY UNNECESSARY WARS

There was a parallel situation on the southern frontier. The Indians in Florida sometimes made raids to the north, and runaway slaves hid out in the swamps and everglades. Further, East Florida was claimed by Spain, then an ally of Britain in the Peninsular War. Leaders in Georgia and Tennessee saw war with Britain and Spain as a way to add Florida to their economic empire.[12]

EFFECT OF THE MEDIA ON PUBLIC OPINION

By the year 1812 a number of newspapers, particularly in Kentucky and Ohio, were advocating war against Britain. The Lexington, Kentucky, *Reporter* ran an editorial on January 21, 1812, urging that the administration:

> ...interpose the American arm between the English and their savage allies. This done, the occupation of the Canadas, New Brunswick and Nova-Scotia would give us perpetual concord with the Indians; who would be obliged to depend upon us for supplies of blankets, knives, gun-powder, etc.

On February 12, 1812, the Circleville, Ohio, *Fredonian* declared that the indignant spirits of Americans could be appeased only "by the restoration of our rights, or the conquest of Canada." On April 14, 1812, the *Kentucky Gazette* stated of the British, "Until these civilized allies of our savage neighbors are expelled from our continent, we must expect the frequent recurrence of the late scenes on the Wabash." On May 26, 1812, the *Gazette* added, "Can it be expected that those savage butcheries will have an end until we take possession of Malden and other British forts on the Lakes?"[13]

Public opinion was outraged by Indian attacks and believed that the British were responsible for them. These editorials undoubtedly reflected popular views.

POLITICAL FACTORS LEADING TO WAR

In the time of George Washington and John Adams, the dominant political party was the Federalists. Thomas Jefferson disagreed with various aspects of the Federalist foreign and domestic policies, and his supporters formed a group known as the Jeffersonian Republicans. Their strength was in the South and West, where agriculture rather than mercantile trade was the dominant economic interest. After Jefferson's election as President in 1800, with the exception of two short intervals, this group remained in power for the next sixty years. However, the Jeffersonians later split into two parties, the Democratic Republicans under Andrew Jackson and the National Republicans under John Quincy Adams and Henry Clay (who soon changed their name to the Whigs). The Democratic Republicans shortened their name to Democrats, thereby causing difficulties for generations of high-school history students. In any case, during the period prior to the War of 1812, the party later known as the Democrats was still known as the Republicans.

In the election of 1808, James Madison, the choice of Thomas Jefferson, received the nomination of the Republicans; Charles Pinckney headed the Federalist ticket. In the Electoral College, Madison received 122 out of 176 votes for President, and George Clinton of New York was chosen as Vice President. However, the Republicans were not united. In 1811, a bill sponsored by the northern Republicans to raise sufficient armed forces to conquer Canada was defeated by a coalition of Federalists and southern Republicans, who feared that the addition of Canada would strengthen the North to the prejudice of southern interests. On the other hand, the northern Republicans had no great enthusiasm for the conquest of Florida.

There was also division on the question of impressment of American seamen. As in the case of interference with U.S. trade by the British, the main effect of the impressment of American seamen was felt in New England.

However, the Beards say, "Northern shipowners, upon whom the losses fell with special weight, did not ask for armed intervention. On the contrary, they took great pains to prove that the federal government's report listing thousands of impressment outrages was false, and they were almost unanimous in their opposition to drawing the sword against England."[14] The shipowners saw, correctly, that the adverse effect of war on their shipping would be far greater than from the acts of the British or French while we remained neutral. Most of the northern Republicans as well as the Federalists, who were strong in New England, were thus antiwar doves. The Madison Republicans in the South and the West, on the other hand, regarded the impressment of our seamen as an affront to the national honor and a sufficient cause for war.

The year 1812 was an election year. As noted above, Madison faced not only opposition from the Federalists but also dissension in the Republican party. Factional groups in the Republican party often joined with the Federalists. These dissident Republicans with some Federalist views included the Old Republicans, led by John Randolph of Virginia; the Clintonians, led by George and De Witt Clinton of New York State; and a Smith faction, led by Samuel Smith of Maryland.[15]

A separate group of Republicans strongly opposed the Federalists. Known as the War Hawks, their leader was Henry Clay of Kentucky. Clay was born in Virginia in 1777 and studied law in Richmond, passing his examination for admission to the bar at the age of twenty. He then moved to Lexington, Kentucky, and was soon licensed to practice law there. He quickly achieved a wide reputation by winning a series of both civil and criminal cases. In his court appearances, he was noted for his rich, melodious voice and his theatrical talent. These abilities also were to prove valuable when Clay entered politics, which he did by being elected to the Kentucky General Assembly in 1803. In 1806 he spent four months in Washington filling out the unexpired term of a senator who had resigned, even though at the age of twenty-nine Clay was below the minimum age of thirty established by the Constitution. He went back to the Kentucky assembly and during 1807 made a number of speeches expressing outrage at the *Chesapeake* incident, in which the British frigate *Leopard* had fired on the U.S. warship when it refused to stop and be searched for British deserters. By 1808 he had risen to become speaker of the lower house. During this period, Clay fought and was wounded in a duel with a man named Humphrey Marshall, who had called him a "poltroon" (which the dictionary defines as "spiritless coward"). In January 1810, Clay was again elected to complete the term of a U.S. senator who had resigned. In contrast to his brief previous term as a senator, Clay now had an opportunity to participate in important debates. In one of his first speeches, he agitated for the conquest of Canada, stating, "The militia of Kentucky alone are competent to place Montreal and Upper Canada at your feet." He also was responsible for a bill authorizing the President to occupy West Florida. However, an indication of the relative importance of the Senate and House of Representatives in those days is that Clay resigned his Senate seat in 1811 to run for Representative, winning easily. He then was elected Speaker of the House of Representatives on the first day of the new session. As the acknowledged leader of the War Hawks, Clay was responsible for passage of a proposal to increase the army by 25,000 men.[16]

Another leader of the War Hawk faction was John C. Calhoun of South Carolina. He was largely self-educated and entered Yale College as a member of the junior class in 1802. Two years later, he graduated from Yale with highest honors and entered the practice of law in Abbeville, South Carolina. When news of the attack on the frigate *Chesapeake* in 1807 reached Abbeville, Calhoun was asked to draw up a resolution condemning the act, to be presented at a public meeting. This he did eloquently, and he was soon elected to the South Carolina state legislature. In 1811 he was elected to Congress by a landslide vote. He immediately formed an alliance with Henry Clay. Although a freshman legislator, Calhoun became chairman of the important Committee on Foreign Relations. A Foreign Relations Committee report, largely the work of Calhoun, called for 50,000 volunteers, the arming of all merchant ships, and the outfitting of warships. Echoing Clay's sentiments in a speech on March 6, 1812, Calhoun stated, "So far from being unprepared, Sir, I believe that in four weeks from the time a declaration of war is heard on our frontier, the whole of upper Canada and a part of lower Canada will be in our power."[17]

Although both Henry Clay and John Calhoun made speeches advocating the conquest of Canada, their prowar sentiment probably stemmed more from their outrage at Britain's insults to the United States than from territorial ambitions. Clay's willingness to fight a duel to avenge a personal insult to his honor was probably indicative of a similar sensitivity to insults to the national honor. Both Clay and Calhoun were particularly impressed by the *Chesapeake* incident, and both felt it would take a war to bring the United States the respect it deserved.

In opposition to the War Hawks were the Federalists, who, as mentioned above, wished to avoid war with Britain because of the effect of conflict on the mercantile interests of their New England constituents. Also opposed to war was a group in the Republican party known as the Quids. Their leader was John Randolph, an eccentric congressman from Virginia. He often appeared on the floor of the House dressed in riding clothes and accompanied by his hunting dogs, which he controlled with a whip. In spite of his appearance, Randolph was an able debater. He condemned the move toward war with Britain as "a churlish submission to Napoleon" that would ruin the country's mercantile trade.

However, his logical arguments against war were no match for the War Hawks' patriotic orations.[18]

THE DECLARATION OF WAR

Madison's biographer John Charles Stagg states, "The President was visited between May 25 and May 29 by a deputation of congressional Republicans headed by Speaker Clay. What they discussed can only be conjectured, but it seems likely that they resumed the earlier discussions that Clay had held with Monroe about the responsibilities of the executive and the legislature in initiating a declaration of war."[19]

In Britain, both the prime minister, Spencer Perceval, and the head of the Foreign Office, Lord Castlereagh, decided to repeal the Orders in Council affecting American trade. Unfortunately, the assassination of Perceval delayed the announcement until June 16, 1812. Had there been a transatlantic cable, war probably could have been averted. However, Congress declared war on June 18, several weeks before the news of the repeal reached Washington.[20]

President Madison was a cautious man, and he probably would have preferred continuing negotiations rather than going to war. However, if he rejected Speaker Clay's proposals, he would in effect be siding with the Federalists and that branch of the Republican party that supported his Republican rival, De Witt Clinton. Particularly in an election year, his choice was clear. On June 1, 1812, Madison sent the members of the Twelfth Congress a message asking them to consider a declaration of war. According to the historian Kendrick Babcock, the message from Madison to Congress "was the sign of Madison's complete surrender to the war party."[21]

In view of the controversy at the time of the Gulf War over the relative roles of the President and Congress in initiating a war, Madison's message is especially interesting. It concludes,

PROBABLY UNNECESSARY WARS

> Whether the United States shall remain passive under these progressive usurpations and these accumulating wrongs, or, opposing force to force in defense of their national rights....is a solemn question which the Constitution wisely confides to the legislative department of the Government. In recommending it to their deliberations, I am happy in the assurance that the decision will be worthy the enlightened and patriotic councils of a virtuous, a free, and a powerful nation.[22]

The House of Representatives met behind closed doors to consider the message, with all visitors and newspaper reporters excluded. The Federalists wanted a public debate, but the Republicans feared the vigorous lobbying against war that might ensue. Apparently there were no major leaks about the debate. The historian Robert Rutland states, "The leading newspaper in Washington simply told readers that an important matter was before Congress." The declaration of war was passed on June 4, 1812, by the House by a vote of seventy-nine to forty-nine and sent to the Senate. Most of the votes against the war came from the Northeast. There followed twelve days of debate in the Senate, also behind closed doors, before the declaration passed nineteen to thirteen.[23]

Madison's message to Congress mentioned violation of U.S. territorial waters and the impressment of American seamen, as well as the presumed aid by the British to the Indians on the frontier. He did not mention the desire for conquest of territory in Canada and Florida, nor did he point out his political motivations. However, by the time war came, these latter two were probably the most important causes. In contrast to his predecessor, Thomas Jefferson, who resisted pressures to go to war after the serious *Chesapeake* incident, James Madison appears to have given more consideration to his own political interests than to the national interest.

OUTCOME OF THE WAR

Negotiations to end the war commenced in Ghent, Belgium, in August 1814 between a British delegation and a strong U.S. team consisting of John Quincy Adams, Ambassador to Russia; Albert Gallatin, Secretary of the Treasury; Henry Clay, Speaker of the House; James Bayard, a Federalist; and Jonathan Russell, a Rhode Island merchant. The British in their opening terms insisted that the Indians be given a permanent reservation carved out of the Northwest Territory, that Britain be ceded land in Maine and Minnesota, and that the Great Lakes be demilitarized. The Americans demanded an end to impressment and blockades, as well as indemnity for losses suffered by U.S. private citizens during the war. After protracted negotiations, the treaty finally signed by the negotiating teams on December 14, 1814, met neither the initial demands of the British nor those of the Americans. It essentially restored territorial boundaries existing before the war, with provision for a commission to settle disputes. There was no mention of impressment or blockade, nor of a neutral Indian territory. The treaty was ratified by the Senate on February 16, 1815.[24]

The official casualty figures for the war were 2,260 killed and 4,505 wounded. Including those who died from disease and accidents related to the war, the total was probably about 20,000. The cost of the war, excluding property damage and lost economic opportunities, was about $160 million.[25]

One of the effects of the war was a strangulation of trade because of the British blockade. The historian Kendrick Babcock states, "By October, 1813, the blockade of the American coast south of Cape Cod was so effective that not a single American man-of-war was free to protect the American coast, and scarcely a vessel flying the American flag was able to enter or leave a port." This had such a severe adverse effect on merchants in New York and

Philadelphia that many were forced out of business. My great-great-grandfather, Isaac Jackson, who had been a successful merchant in New York City, decided to close his failing business and move to Ohio, where he became a farmer.

WHAT IF THIS WAR HAD NOT TAKEN PLACE?

The previous section pointed out the adverse effect of the British blockade on merchants in the Northeast and in the New England states. The historian Donald Hickey states, "Unlike most American wars, this one did not generate a general economic boom." If war had not been declared, after the British revoked their Orders in Council, the economy probably would have continued its rise.

The war also obviously soured United States-Canadian relations. To this day, the United States still has a naval presence in the Great Lakes, including a frigate stationed at the Soo Canals, presumably to protect us in case of renewed hostilities with Canada. In the absence of war, which tended to increase nationalistic feelings on both sides, there would have been strong pressures for political union between the two countries. There were thousands of Loyalists in Canada who had fled the Colonies at the time of the Revolution, plus many more settlers who had taken advantage of Canadian offers of free land. Without the enmity between the two nations induced by war, the political pressure of these former Americans might have led to a strong unification sentiment.

WAS THIS WAR NECESSARY?

There were two times before the War of 1812 when the issue of peace and war hung in the balance. The first was when the British announced the suspension of the Orders in Council, which set up the system of blockades and licenses, two days before the United States declared war. Unfortunately, the news did not reach Washington for another two weeks. If a transatlantic cable had existed or if the Madison Administration had possessed more patience and fortitude in standing up to the War Hawks, war might have been averted. The debate in Congress on the declaration of war also could have gone either way. During the Senate debate, a motion to amend the declaration so that it merely authorized naval vessels to make reprisals against Britain passed by a vote of seventeen to thirteen, only to have the modified bill defeated three days later in a tie vote broken by the President Pro Tem.[26] The Senate deliberations behind closed doors lasted two weeks; a debate open to the public might have led to a different outcome.

At this point, it is probably worth reviewing the criteria used in this book to decide whether a war was necessary or not. In Chapter I, we defined a war as unnecessary if

A. it failed to achieve any of the aims which led to the declaration of war, OR IF
B. the war did achieve its aims initially, but these proved to be short-lived, OR IF
C. The aims could have been achieved without resort to war.

In his message to Congress asking for a declaration of war against Britain, President Madison cited the impressment of American seamen, the blockading of U.S. ports, violations of U.S. territorial waters, and British influence on the Indians in the Northwest. Not listed, but more important than any of these to some of the War Hawks was the conquest of Canada. As noted in the previous section, the United States failed to achieve any of these goals. First and foremost, it failed in its aim to conquer Canada and free that country from British control. It also failed to secure from the British in the peace treaty any guarantees against the future impressment of seamen or blockade of American ports. Thus, the War of 1812 falls under category A above.

PROBABLY UNNECESSARY WARS

History also shows that most of the aims would have been secured if the United States had pursued a policy of patient neutrality until the European wars ended. Even though the British gave no guarantees against the impressment of American seamen, they ceased the practice anyway. With the end of the Napoleonic Wars, the British navy no longer needed the crews. The end of the European wars also brought an end to blockades and the harassment of American vessels. Since the end of the Napoleonic Wars was entirely independent of the resolution of the American conflict, it is virtually certain that impressment and harassment of American shipping by the British would have ended anyway. Thus, the War of 1812 was also unnecessary under category C above.

If one takes a long enough view, one can even argue that the economic conquest of Canada was eventually achieved without war. The 1992 trade agreements, which virtually eliminate tariff barriers, have the effect of adding the Canadian market to the U.S. economy. Henry Clay could not have asked for anything more!

However, this is not to say that the War of 1812 had no effect on subsequent U.S. history. As the introductory chapter pointed out, a war can be unnecessary but still be profoundly influential. The War of 1812 did succeed in unifying the Republican party, leading to an era of one-party rule. More important, the war unified the country and brought about a consciousness and pride in American nationality. The war also succeeded in bringing a recognition by the French and the British that America was no longer a semicolonial dependency but a first-class, independent nation. These were important changes that probably would not have occurred in this time period in the absence of war. However, they are in the nature of "side effects" and do not form a justification for starting the war.

Thus, my conclusion is that the War of 1812 was probably unnecessary but nevertheless was a significant influence in shaping America's future.

Chapter III

THE SPANISH-AMERICAN WAR

C uba was visited by Christopher Columbus during his first voyage in 1492, and he claimed possession for Spain. By the latter part of the nineteenth century, Cuba was one of the few Spanish possessions left in the New World. After largely wiping out the native population, the Spaniards turned to African slaves for their labor force. Even after slavery was abolished in the latter half of the nineteenth century, Spanish rule was harsh. The populace revolted in 1868 in a futile struggle that lasted ten years. A new revolt started in 1895, led by the poet-revolutionary José Martí. Although Martí died in an early skirmish, his fellow revolutionists continued the struggle, employing guerrilla-warfare tactics. They also embarked on a campaign to burn the Spanish sugar plantations.

The United States had long had an interest in Cuba. In 1854, prior to the Cuban revolts, President Franklin Pierce asked his Secretary of State to find out the opinion of American ambassadors to Spain, France, and Britain on the question of Cuba. They met in Ostend, Belgium, and drafted a document (known as The Ostend Manifesto) that strongly recommended the annexation of Cuba by either purchase or force. The document was supposed to have been kept confidential but was leaked to the London press. President

Pierce refused to endorse it, but the idea had a fair amount of support, particularly in the southern states.[1]

Forty years later, the American public was split on the question of foreign expansion. A substantial number of voters supported the doctrine of Manifest Destiny. This doctrine was originally applied to the inevitability of the expansion of the United States on the North American Continent, but by the 1890s, Manifest Destiny was also applied to expansion in the Caribbean and the Pacific. The principle issue in the presidential campaign of 1896 between Democrat William Jennings Bryan and Republican William McKinley was Bryan's demand for free silver (a policy that the government would purchase all silver offered at a ratio of sixteen ounces of silver to one ounce of gold). However, imperialism in the form of manifest destiny was a subsidiary issue. Most Democrats at that time were anti-imperialist, whereas many prominent Republicans were expansionist.

SPANISH ACTS INFLAMING AMERICAN PUBLIC OPINION

As was the case in the War of 1812, the potential adversary, this time Spain, committed a number of actions that adversely aroused American public opinion.

Spanish Mistreatment of Cuban Revolutionaries

The Spanish general Aleriano Weyler responded to the Martí uprising of 1895 by rounding up the peasants and placing them in concentration camps. Conditions were horrible—no beds, toilet facilities, or medical attention, and a severe shortage of food. Probably one quarter of the Cuban population, 400,000 people, died because of the concentration camps and other policies instituted by General Weyler. A group of Cuban sympathizers in New York City made sure that the American public was made aware of these atrocities.[2]

Responding to the public outcry. President McKinley lodged protests with the Spanish government. Spain recalled General Weyler, disbanded the concentration camps, and indicated its willingness to make further concessions to avoid war.

The Sinking of the Battleship *Maine*

In March 1895, a Spanish gunboat fired shots across the bow of the American steamer *Aliança* while it was sailing in the Windward Passage between Cuba and Haiti. The commanding officer of the gunboat believed that the *Aliança* had been trying to land arms for the Cuban rebels and said that the ship was in Cuban waters, which the Americans denied. No harm was done, but this incident was played up by the press and led to speeches in Congress.

There were some further incidents, and by early 1898 tensions had risen on both sides. The American consul-general in Havana, Fitzhugh Lee, requested that the battleship *Maine* be sent to Havana, and on January 24, 1898, it left Key West for Havana. The first three weeks that the *Maine* was in Havana passed peacefully. The officers were wined and dined by the Cuban authorities, and they wined and dined them in return. The captain of the *Maine*, Charles Sigsbee, even went to a bullfight.[3] Then on the night of February 15, the ship blew up.

To this day, there has been no agreement on the cause of the blast. A U.S. Navy board of inquiry blamed the sinking on a mine explosion outside the forward magazine, The report of the board of inquiry did not assign blame for the mine, but New York City newspapers quickly planted responsibility with the Spanish. The newspapers and the public chose to ignore the facts that the Spanish had no reason to plant the mine, quickly sent messages of condolence, and asked for an international inquiry. Some later historians have suggested that the rebels might have done it, but it is doubtful that they had the equipment or expertise. In 1976, Admiral Hyman G. Rickover, who is best known as "the father of the nuclear Navy," wrote a book called *How the Battleship* Maine *Was Destroyed*. Rickover argued that the battleship was destroyed by an internal explosion triggered by a smoldering coal fire in a sealed bunker adjacent to an ammunition magazine.[4] Since the *Maine* was later refloated, towed out of Havana harbor, and sunk in deep water, there probably never will be a definitive answer.

Nevertheless, the sinking, which led to the slogan "Remember the *Maine*!", was a major factor in provoking the war.

ECONOMIC FACTORS LEADING TO PRESSURE FOR WAR

By the time of William McKinley's election to the Presidency, Cuban-American trade was approximately $100 million annually, and American investments were more than $50 million. Realizing the effect that their action would have on the attitude of certain American circles towards intervention, the Cuban rebels deliberately destroyed many sugar plantations.[5] American investors in these plantations reacted predictably in demanding that the United States protect of their property.

The historian Samuel Eliot Morrison gives another economic reason for the war: "The Dingley tariff of 1897 [which raised rates on wool, hides, flax, silk and linen] was the highest protective tariff that had yet been enacted. So blatant were the monopoly-securing features of this tariff that the Republican party was badly in need of a new issue to divert popular attention. Cuba provided the diversion."[6]

EFFECT OF THE MEDIA ON PUBLIC OPINION

In the 1890s, the two leading sensationalist newspapers in New York City were Joseph Pulitzer's *World* and William Randolph Hearst's *Journal*. Because the yellow color used in their comic strips often smeared, they were known as the yellow press. In their journalistic wars for circulation, the papers often manufactured their own crusades. Both newspapers decided to cover the Cuban war in depth, including sketches of the military action. Some of the artists employed to make these sketches, such as Frederic Remington, were nationally known. When Remington asked Hearst's permission to return to New York, since there was no war, Hearst replied:

> Remington
> Havana
> Please remain. You furnish the pictures and I will furnish the war.
> — William Randolph Hearst[7]

The reporters included the young Winston Churchill, who reported accurately for the *World*, but many of his fellow reporters let their imagination roam rather freely. Gunshots in the distance became "volleys fired by jailers as they murdered defenseless prisoners."[8]

The competition between the *Journal* and the *World* produced some striking banner headlines, such as that in Hearst's *Journal* on February 9, 1898: "Worst Insult to the United States in History." The insult referred to was contained in a private letter from the Spanish ambassador, Enrique Dupuy de Lôme, to a friend, the editor of the Madrid *Heraldo*, who was visiting Cuba. The letter was intercepted by a Cuban spy, photographed, and a copy sent to Hearst. The letter, as translated, commented that President McKinley was a "cheap politician who truckled to the masses."[9]

The publication of the letter was followed a week later by the sinking of the *Maine*. The *World* sent a special tug with its own divers to make an inquiry, but there was never any question in either the *World* or *Journal* that Spain was at fault; the only unresolved point was whether the deed had been done by a mine or a torpedo. In response to continuing press coverage, Spanish flags were burned by crowds demanding vengeance. Visitors to the House and Senate galleries sat wrapped in American flags, demanding war.[10] Since President McKinley did not immediately press for war, the press and many politicians turned on him. Some of their remarks made de Lome's comments in his private letter seem almost like compliments. Theodore Roosevelt, then Assistant Secretary of the Navy, was reported to have said, "The President has no more backbone than a chocolate eclair."[11]

POLITICAL FACTORS LEADING TO WAR

Prior to his nomination as the Republican candidate for President in 1896, William McKinley had served fourteen years in Congress and two terms as governor of Ohio. During his terms in Congress, he supported the manufacturers of Ohio by drafting and enacting a protective tariff in 1890, which was known as the McKinley Tariff. At that time, one of the most powerful men in the Republican party was an Ohio businessman named Marcus Hanna. Hanna made large personal contributions to secure McKinley's nomination for President in 1896 and was manager of his campaign.[12] As a businessman, Hanna hoped that McKinley would bring four years of peace and stability. He is quoted by the historian Thomas Beer as having said, "The United States must not have any damn trouble with anybody."[13]

Among the appointments of President McKinley after his election in 1896 were John D. Long, a gentleman farmer from Maine, as Secretary of the Navy and Theodore Roosevelt, then New York City Police Commissioner, as his assistant.

Theodore Roosevelt was born in 1858 in New York City to a wealthy family that dated back to the early Dutch in New Amsterdam. As a boy, he was sickly, nearsighted, and asthmatic. However, as a teenager he determined to build his body through a program of rigorous exercise, and he succeeded. He was educated with private tutors and entered Harvard College in 1876, graduating magna cum laude in 1880. He was elected to the prestigious Porcellian club. After graduation, he entered Columbia Law School, and in his spare time not only worked for the local Republican party but also started writing a book, *The Naval War of 1812* (which was one of the sources used in the previous chapter). In 1881 at the age of twenty-three he was nominated for the New York State Assembly, and he won the resulting election by a large margin. In that same year he completed his naval history. His research for the book convinced him that the U.S. Navy of 1881 was relatively inferior to the navy of 1812. In his preface, he stated, "It is folly...to rely for defense upon a Navy composed partly of antiquated hulks and partly of new vessels rather more worthless than the old." Meanwhile, in the Assembly, he quickly established a reputation as a reformer. In 1883, while still the youngest man in the legislature. his nomination by his Republican colleagues for the position of speaker was approved by acclamation. Although he lost the subsequent election to the Democratic candidate for speaker, he was still minority leader. During the following session he worked with the Democratic governor, Grover Cleveland, to pass a civil service reform bill. In 1884, Roosevelt was elected a delegate to the national Republican convention, where he spent considerable time with a delegate from Massachusetts, Henry Cabot Lodge.[14]

Henry Cabot Lodge was born in Boston, Massachusetts, in 1850 to a wealthy family and, like Theodore Roosevelt, attended Harvard College and was elected to Porcellian. He graduated in 1871, received a law degree in 1874, and was granted Harvard's first Ph.D. degree in political science in 1876. After teaching American history at Harvard for several years, he entered politics. By the time of the 1884 Republican convention, he had served two terms in the Massachusetts House of Representatives, was chairman of the Massachusetts Republican party, and a candidate for Congress. Lodge was the author of biographies of Alexander Hamilton and Daniel Webster. He shared with

Roosevelt not only authorship, wealth, and membership in Porcellian at Harvard but also, according to the historian Edmund Morris,"a massive ego and a ruthless ambition."[15]

Roosevelt returned to New York City and ran for the office of mayor in a three-way contest that included Henry George, a radical economist famous for his book *Progress and Poverty*. Roosevelt was badly defeated but was partly consoled by the news that his friend Henry Cabot Lodge had been elected to the Congress of the United States. In 1889, Lodge secured Roosevelt's appointment by President Benjamin Harrison to the U.S. Civil Service Commission. After six years in that agency, he was appointed by a reform New York mayor, William Strong, as New York City Police Commissioner. Then, after both Roosevelt and Lodge had been active in the Presidential campaign of William McKinley, Lodge was instrumental in securing Roosevelt's appointment as Assistant Secretary of the Navy.

Lodge and Roosevelt had one additional thing in common—both were admirers of Captain Alfred Thayer Mahan, whose book *The Influence of Sea Power Upon History* made a strong case that sea power decided the fate of nations and empires. Mahan argued that a nation needed both a battle fleet to protect its merchant ships and coastal cities and also overseas bases for repairing and refueling the warships. Both Lodge and Roosevelt accepted Mahan's thesis that a large modern navy and a dominant influence in the Caribbean and Pacific were vital to the security of the United States.

According to Roosevelt's biographer Edmund Morris, Secretary of the Navy John D. Long "was by nature indolent." He much preferred his country home in Hingham Harbor, Massachusetts, to Washington and took extended summer vacations.[16]

Roosevelt took advantage of these absences. While Long was in New England on vacation in September 1897, Roosevelt intercepted a letter from Senator William Chandler recommending that Long appoint Commodore John Howell to head up the Asiatic Fleet. Roosevelt felt that Howell was not sufficiently aggressive and, before Long returned, arranged that President McKinley should recommend the appointment of Commodore George Dewey, Roosevelt's choice, as commander of the Asiatic Fleet. Dewey assumed command in October 1897. Following the sinking of the *Maine* in February 1898, Secretary Long again was away from the office, this time to visit a doctor. While he was out, Roosevelt met with his friend Henry Cabot Lodge. They agreed on a plan of action, and Roosevelt immediately ordered large new supplies of ammunition to put the navy on war footing. Roosevelt cabled Dewey:

> "Order the squadron...to Hong Kong. Keep full of coal. In the event of declaration of war [with] Spain, your duty will be to see that the Spanish squadron does not leave the Asiatic coast and then [to under-take] offensive operations in Philippine Islands."[17].

When he returned to the office, Long verified the order, and eventually President McKinley was told of the plan.

Although Roosevelt and Lodge were the leaders of the prowar faction in the McKinley Administration, they had the support of other influential senators, including William Chandler and James Donald Cameron. Among those working for peace were the American ambassador to Spain, Stewart L. Woodward, and Mark Hanna, by then a Republican senator. At a Gridiron Club dinner, where both Roosevelt and Hanna were present, Hanna made an antiwar speech. In his reply, Roosevelt stated, "We will have this war with Cuba, Senator Hanna, in spite of the timidity of the commercial interests!" Roosevelt continued to be disturbed by McKinley's efforts to find a diplomatic solution to the crisis. His biographer Nathan Miller reports him as saying, "Do you know what that white-faced cur up there has done? He has prepared two messages, one for war and one for peace, and he doesn't know which one to send in!"[18] Most of the Democratic senators favored negotiation rather than war. However, the hawks outnumbered the doves.

William McKinley was the last American President to have served in the Civil War. He once told a friend, "I have been through one war. I have seen the dead piled up, and I do not want to see another."[19] Initially, McKinley seemed to be following the policy of his predecessor, Grover Cleveland, who had resisted pressures for war with Spain during his Administration.

However, in the spring of 1898, McKinley's feelings about war seem to have been influenced by the upcoming congressional elections in November 1898. The historian James Ford Rhodes states: "McKinley feared a rupture in his own party, and on account of that fear, had not the nerve and power to resist the pressure for war. We may rest assured that if Mark Hanna had been President there would have been no war with Spain. As much of a partisan as McKinley, he would have had the self-determination to resist the war party and the confident belief that he could secure the end desired without war and without the rupture of the Republican party; at all events he would have taken the risk."[20] It also seems likely the Grover Cleveland would have resisted war pressures if he had still been serving as President, since he did so during his Administration.

THE DECLARATION OF WAR

The American ambassador to Spain, Stewart L. Woodford, cabled McKinley on April 10, 1898, that the Madrid government was willing to grant Cuba autonomy or complete independence. Woodford said that Spain would even cede the island to the United States. The same day the Spanish minister in Washington confirmed that the his government had ordered a cessation of hostilities, revoked the order for reconcentration, and agreed to an autonomous government for Cuba.[21] However, McKinley was committed to a course leading to war and sent a message to Congress the next day. McKinley himself said a year later, "But for the inflamed state of public opinion, and the fact that Congress could no longer be held in check, a peaceful solution might have been had."[22]

In his April 11, 1898, war message to Congress, the President recounted the events which in his mind justified intervention in Cuba. The historian Henry Steele Commanger commented on the message: "Filled with suggestion and innuendo, the account is thoroughly misleading, but it struck a responsive note in Congress and in the public mind. In as much as Spain, in the note received by McKinley April 10, promised to order an immediate cessation of hostilities in Cuba, the principal basis for intervention had disappeared."[23] The House quickly passed a resolution authorizing armed intervention. The corresponding Senate resolution also urged recognition of the Cuban republic. In the Senate, the anti-imperialists succeeded in getting a declaration that "The United States hereby disclaims any disposition or intention to exercise sovereignty, jurisdiction or control over said Island except for the pacification thereof, and asserts its determination, when that is accomplished, to leave the government and control of the Island to its people." This became known as the Teller Amendment, after its sponsor, Senator Henry F. Teller of Colorado. There was no corresponding statement with respect to the Philippines, Guam, or Puerto Rico.[24]

A conference committee took nearly a week to reconcile the bills, with the key step being the Teller Amendment disclaiming any desire for sovereignty over Cuba. McKinley signed the joint resolution on April 20, 1898, and Congress passed a formal declaration of war five days later. In neither of these documents was there any mention of Puerto Rico or the Philippines.

Of the possible causes of war listed in this chapter, President McKinley mentioned three—sympathy with the Cuban people's desire for independence, concern about American investments in Cuba, and Spanish actions against U.S. citizens and interests. He did not point out the territorial desires of some officials in his Administration and his own political motives. However, as in the case of the War of 1812, these latter two were probably paramount in bringing about the actual declaration.

OUTCOME OF THE WAR

In late July 1898, the French ambassador in Washington, Jules Gabon, who was representing Spain, put out a peace feeler, and a protocol of agreement was signed on August 12. Later that fall, McKinley appointed a peace commission to meet in Paris with its Spanish counterpart. In the treaty that was signed in Paris on December 10, 1898, Spain relinquished all claims to Cuba and ceded Puerto Rico, Guam, and the Philippines to the United States. For the Philippines, the United States paid Spain $20 million.

The official casualty figures from the war were 385 battle deaths and 2,061 other deaths (Department of Defense figures.) The estimated cost of the war was $283 million, excluding interest on the debt and veterans' benefits. These do not include the casualties or costs of the subsequent war to subjugate the Philippines.

After the war, the United States insisted that Cuba incorporate in its constitution a series of restrictions that limited the relations of Cuba with foreign countries, granted the use of Guantanamo Bay for a U.S. naval base, and gave the United States the right to interfere in Cuban internal affairs to protect life and property. These conditions are known as the Platt Amendment after Senator Orville H. Platt of Connecticut, who proposed them.[25] The amendment was invoked in 1906, when the United States sent the marines to Cuba to help restore order.

PROBABLY UNNECESSARY WARS

Following the peace with Spain, the United States decided to extend its authority over the Philippines in spite of opposition of the rebels led by the patriot Emilio Aguinaldo. Although the rebels were defeated in a battle near Manila in February 1899, it took three more years of struggle against guerrilla warfare to complete the subjugation. About 1,000 more American casualties ensued.

WHAT IF THIS WAR HAD NOT TAKEN PLACE?
As noted above, Spain had agreed to a cessation of hostilities in Cuba and the grant of a measure of self-government shortly before President McKinley sent his war message to Congress. Thus, even without war, Cuba would likely have soon achieved self-government in a sort of dominion arrangement under Spain. Because of the weakness of Spain in the early twentieth century, full independence would have soon followed. In this case, Cuba would not have been encumbered with American interference imposed by the Teller Amendment nor by the U.S. presence at Guantanamo naval base.

If the war had not taken place, there would have been no basis for the U.S. acquisition of the Philippines, Guam, or Puerto Rico. In the Philippines, it is very likely that the revolt against Spanish rule led by Aguinaldo would have succeeded, since it took the full power of the U.S. Army three years to suppress it. Puerto Rico also probably would have become an independent republic similar to the Dominican Republic. Whether the net effect of independence rather than American rule would have been positive for the people of the Philippines and Puerto Rico depends on one's views of colonialism.

WAS THIS WAR NECESSARY?
Before President McKinley sent his war message to Congress, he had received the news from Ambassador Woodford that Spain had agreed to virtually all of the

American demands. (The exception was that Spain wanted the rebels to initiate an armistice, with which they assured Woodford they would comply.) Thus, if the President had taken a strong stand that we had won our objectives in Cuba without hostilities, there need not have been a war. Since the vote in the Senate on the war resolution was relatively close (41 for, 35 against, with 12 abstentions),[26] it is doubtful that Congress would have declared war without the President's prowar message.

From the American point of view, the Spanish-American War was successful. It accomplished both our stated aim of freeing Cuba from Spanish domination and our unstated aim of imperial expansion into Puerto Rico and the Philippines.

However, as noted above, it is almost certain that Cuba could have achieved independence without American assistance. After all, Spain had offered Cuba limited self-rule before war was declared. As for the colonial conquests, with the hindsight of history, it seems questionable that the acquisition of the Philippines and Puerto Rico were net pluses for the United States. Thus, although the war did advance McKinley's political interests and helped ensure his reelection in 1900, it seems dubious that it really was in the national interest to suffer the expense and the loss of lives resulting from the war with Spain. Thus, I would classify this war as probably unnecessary.

If the war was unnecessary, why did it take place? The answers, I believe, are similar to those of why the War of 1812 took place. First, there was a series of real or imagined provocations by the adversary, Spain, culminating in the sinking of the battleship *Maine*. The provocations were reported (and exaggerated) by the press, leading to a public outcry for action. Congressmen and senators responded to the pressure from their constituents, as well from hawks such as Theodore Roosevelt in the Administration. President

PROBABLY UNNECESSARY WARS

McKinley was not strong enough to withstand these pressures and provide the leadership necessary to preserve the peace.

Chapter IV

THE VIETNAM WAR

*T*he Vietnam War differs from other wars in this book in that there never was a formal declaration of war by the Congress of the United States. Thus, there is not the usual dividing point between events leading up to a war and the war itself. For purposes of this book, this dividing point will be considered the Tonkin Gulf resolution passed by Congress after President Lyndon Johnson announced that two United States destroyers had been attacked in international waters off Vietnam by North Vietnamese torpedo boats. The resolution, passed on August 7, 1964, declared the support by the Congress of the President in all efforts to repel armed attack on U. S. forces.[1] This resolution was subsequently used by the Administration as basic legislative approval for all of its actions in the prosecution of the war. Consequently, this chapter will summarize the historical background and the reasons for U. S. involvement in the Vietnam conflict up to the Gulf of Tonkin incident and then move to the outcome of the war.

HISTORICAL BACKGROUND[2]

Before World War II, the area in the Indochinese peninsula that later became Vietnam was divided into three separate units. The south, called Cochin China, was conquered by the French in a series of campaigns between 1858 and 1867 and established as a colony, with its capital in Saigon. It was a rich, agricultural land and exported up to two million tons of rice annually. The central area was established as a protectorate in 1884, rather than a colony. It kept the old name of Annam and had its capital in Hue. The territory of Tonkin in the north, with its capital in Hanoi, was also established as a protectorate in 1884, though a number of offices of the Government-General of French Indochina were located there. Tonkin was a net importer of rice, with many of its peasants going south to seek employment. French Indochina included these three parts of Vietnam, plus Cambodia and Laos, which also were protectorates. Although French policy was to consider Cochin China, Amman, and Tonkin as separate administrative units, they left the Vietnamese emperor, who claimed sovereignty over all three territories, in place. However, he had little actual power.

After the Japanese conquered Indochina in World War II, they stationed garrisons there but ruled through the existing French colonial administration, leaving Vietnamese Emperor Bao Dai, as well as the rulers of Cambodia and Laos, on their thrones. In March 1945 as the Allied forces approached Indochina, the Japanese took full control from the French in order to forestall moves by French officers to overthrow them. The Japanese ordered Emperor Bao Dai, as well as King Sihanouk of Cambodia and the king of Laos to declare independence for their countries. All three complied.

However, the leader of the Communist resistance in northern Vietnam, Ho Chi Minh. refused to accept Bao Dai's declaration. Ho Chi Minh's forces, known as the Vietminh, seized Hanoi. Power shifted again following the Japanese surrender in August 1945. On August 25, 1945, Bao Dai resigned as emperor at the behest of Ho Chi Minh, and on September 2, 1945, Ho proclaimed the Democratic Republic of Vietnam at Hanoi, reaffirming Vietnam's independence and unity. In his speech, Ho Chi Minh included the words: "We hold the truth that all men are created equal, that they are endowed by their creator with certain inalienable rights, among them life, liberty, and the pursuit of happiness." He told an American OSS (the forerunner of the CIA) agent that he would welcome a million American soldiers, but no French.[3] The West did not reply to this offer.

In the same month of August 1945, the French in Saigon attempted to re-establish their sovereignty. Four years of fighting and negotiation between the French and the Vietminh ensued. In 1948, France decided to complement its military campaign with the political maneuver of establishing a regime in Vietnam that would be "independent within the French Union." The French persuaded Emperor Bao Dai to head up a state that nominally included Cochin China, Annam, and Tonkin. Thus the unified state of Vietnam was established in the Elysée agreements, signed in Paris on March 8, 1949. However, under the agreements, France was to maintain control of Vietnam's defense, diplomacy, and finances. Again, Ho Chi Minh did not accept Bao Dai as the legitimate representative of the people of Vietnam. Ho made one last effort to compromise and promised that in the growing conflict between the West and the Communist world, he would guarantee Vietnam's neutrality. The West did not respond, and Ho Chi Minh than persuaded the Soviet Union and China to recognize his regime.

REASONS FOR U.S.INVOLVEMENT IN VIETNAM
Opposition to World Communism

With recognition of Ho Chi Minh's government by the Soviet Union and China, the French successfully portrayed their actions in Vietnam as part of the struggle against world Communism, which was viewed as a monolithic bloc. Concern in the United States over Communism had been increased by the Communist takeover of China in 1949. Dean Acheson, Secretary of State under President Harry Truman, advised the President in March, 1950, to allocate $15 million of discretionary military spending for military aid to France in Indochina. In June 1950, the Assistant Secretary of State for Far Eastern Affairs, Dean Rusk, justified the aid to France as follows in testimony before the Senate Foreign Relations Committee in June, 1950:

> This is a civil war that has in effect been captured by the Soviet Politburo and, besides, has been turned into a tool of the Politburo. So it isn't a civil war in the usual sense. It is part of an international war..... We have to look at it in terms of which side we are on in this particular kind of struggle....Because Ho Chi Minh is tied in with the Politburo, our policy is to support Bao Dai and the French in Indochina until we have time to help them establish a going concern.[4]

However, these views were not universally held. In November 1951, Senator John F. Kennedy declared:

> In Indochina, we have allied ourselves to the desperate efforts of the French regime to hang on to the remnants of Empire. There is no broad, general support of the native (Bao Dai) Vietnam government among the people in that area.[5]

Nevertheless, U.S. financial support for the French in Indochina continued to grow, particularly after the Korean War broke out on June 25, 1950. By the fiscal year 1954, U.S. aid was more than $1 billion, and in April of that year it was announced that aid for the following fiscal year would be $1.33 billion, over one third of the entire U.S. foreign aid program.[6] The French struggle against the Vietminh came to a decisive conclusion at the battle of Dienbienphu. There the French had constructed a very strong fortress defended by heavy artillery. The strategy of French General Henri Navarre was to lure the Vietminh to attack the supposedly impregnable position and then to destroy them. The Vietminh accept

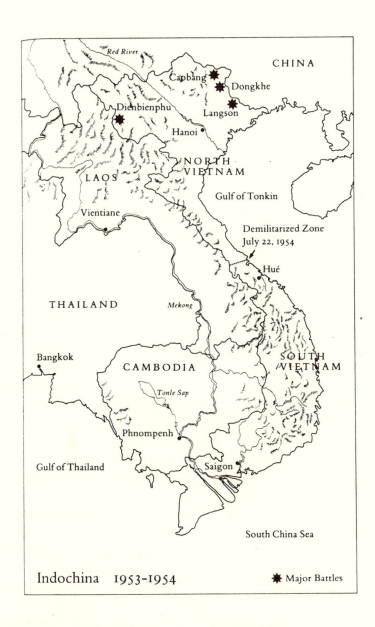

Indochina 1953-1954

★ Major Battles

FRENCH INDOCHINA (From Stanley Karnow's *Vietnam: A History*)

ed the challenge. After positioning about 50,000 troops (compared to 13,000 French defenders), the Vietminh began its attack on March 13, 1954. A week later, the French urgently asked for American assistance. President Dwight Eisenhower refused to supply military aid to the French without the support of Congress and our allies. He told his staff, "Without allies and associates, the leader is just an adventurer, like Genghis Khan."

Accordingly, three supporters of U.S. intervention, Admiral Arthur Radford, Chairman of the Joint Chiefs of Staff, John Foster Dulles, Secretary of State, and Richard Nixon, Vice President, tried to get Congress to approve the use of air power in Vietnam at the President's discretion. The approval was blocked by several key members of Congress, including Senator Lyndon Johnson, then majority leader. In view of Johnson's later involvement in the war, this may seem inconsistent, but it must be remembered that when he next was confronted with the Vietnam question, President John F. Kennedy had already made the decision to support the South Vietnamese with military advisers.

A parallel effort was made to secure support from the British. When Prime Minister Winston Churchill refused to participate, any chance of American help disappeared. The French were decisively defeated on May 7, 1954.[7]

There followed a Geneva Conference on Indochina. The United States attended the conference, but under instructions from President Eisenhower, its representative, Bedell Smith, did not participate in the negotiations. The conference eventually resulted in an armistice agreement on Vietnam signed on July 20, 1954, by representatives of France and the Vietminh. This provided for temporary partition of the country along the 17th parallel, with regrouping of opposing forces to the two zones. The conference also produced a Final Declaration, which endorsed the armistice terms, set up an International Control Commission, and provided for national elections to ensure unification before July 20, 1956. The Final Declaration was approved orally by France, China, the Soviet Union, Great Britain, Laos, Cambodia, and the Vietminh, but not by the United States. The United States did issue a unilateral declaration stating, "We shall continue to seek to achieve unity through free elections, supervised by the United Nations to ensure that they are conducted fairly."[8] However, the representatives of Bao Dai at the conference refused to endorse the declaration. About halfway through the Geneva Conference, Bao Dai appointed as his prime minister Ngo Dinh Diem, a Roman Catholic who had formerly served in his court and subsequently spent four years in the United States. In October 1955, Diem organized a referendum that ousted Bao Dai. The French agreed to withdraw their troops, with the last leaving in April 1956. Diem consolidated all of the South Vietnamese forces under his control. In spite of pressure from the International Control Commission, Diem also refused to consider holding the election provided for in the Geneva agreements. In this refusal, Diem was backed by the United States. Meanwhile, the United States increased both its number of "advisers" and its aid to Diem's government. By 1960 the U.S. Military Assistance Advisory Group (M.A.A.G.) in Vietnam numbered 4,000 Americans.[9]

Following the fiasco at the Bay of Pigs in Cuba in April 1961, President John F. Kennedy linked Cuba and Vietnam in this speech to the American Society of Newspaper Editors:

> It is clear that we face a relentless struggle in every corner of the globe that goes beyond the clash of armies or even nuclear armaments. The armies are there, and in large numbers. The nuclear armaments are there. But they serve primarily as a shield behind which subversion, infiltration, and a host of other tactics steadily advance, picking off vulnerable areas one by one....We dare not fail to see the insidious

nature of this new and deeper struggle. We dare not fail to grasp the new concepts, the new tools, the new sense of urgency we need to combat it — whether in Cuba or South Vietnam.[10]

Shortly thereafter, President Kennedy sent Vice President Lyndon Johnson, on a fact-finding mission to Southeast Asia. His principal conclusion was: "The battle against Communism must be joined in Southeast Asia with strength and determination to achieve success there — or the United States, inevitably, must surrender the Pacific and take up our defenses on our own shores." In the final paragraph of the report, he stated: "The fundamental decision required of the United States — and time is of the greatest importance — is whether we are to attempt to meet the challenge of Communist expansion now in Southeast Asia by a major effort in support of the forces of freedom in the area or throw in the towel."[11] These arguments were later simplified by supporters of the war to the statement, "We either fight the Commies in Vietnam, or on the beaches of California."

The Domino Theory

In a press conference held on April 7, 1954, President Dwight Eisenhower first introduced the "falling domino" principle. In response to a question from the reporter Robert Richards asking him to comment on the strategic importance of Indochina to the free world, the President replied:

Finally, you have broader considerations that might follow what you would call the "falling domino" principle. You have a row of dominoes set up, you knock over the first one, and what will happen to the last one is certainly that it will go over very quickly. So you have a beginning of a disintegration that would have the most profound influences.

When we come to the possible sequence of events, the loss of Indochina, of Burma, of Thailand, of the Peninsula and Indonesia following, now you begin to talk about areas that not only multiply the disadvantages that you would suffer through loss of materials, sources of materials, but now you are really talking about millions and millions and millions of people.[12]

The domino theory also was a strong factor in the decision to commit the first U. S. troops to Vietnam, rather than rely on Vietnamese troops with U.S. advisers. Following Vice President Johnson's visit to Vietnam referred to above, President Kennedy sent General Maxwell Taylor to Saigon in October 1951. In his report on his tour, General Taylor stated that "If Vietnam goes, it will be exceedingly difficult if not impossible to hold Southeast Asia." He urged the deployment of three squadrons of helicopters, manned by American pilots, plus 8,000 U.S. combat troops disguised as engineers to help with the floods in the Mekong Delta.[13] Although the President delayed sending in combat troops, he did approve increasing the number of advisers, which reached 11,000 by the end of 1962 and 23,000 two years later.[14] The United States also sent in helicopter pilots, who eventually began firing at insurgent troops in addition to ferrying Vietnamese soldiers.

Again in 1964, the Joint Chiefs of Staff in a report to President Johnson stated that South Vietnam was pivotal to America's worldwide confrontation with Communism, and a defeat there would be a blow to U.S. "durability, resolution, and trustworthiness" throughout Asia.[15]

United States Credibility

As the U. S. presence in Vietnam grew, the justification for being there increasingly became that Vietnam was a test case in counterinsurgency that the nation could not afford to lose. General Maxwell Taylor, the U.S. ambassador to Saigon, said in 1964, "If we leave Vietnam with our tail between our legs, the consequences of this defeat in the rest of Asia, Africa, and Latin America would be disastrous."[16]

A variation of that view was that if we showed weakness in Vietnam, our allies everywhere would stop trusting U.S. commitments. The United States would be viewed by our adversaries as a "pitiful, helpless giant" or a "paper tiger." If the adversaries were appeased, as Hitler was in the 1930s, their appetites would be whetted for further conquests.[17]

Freedom and Democracy for the South Vietnamese

The three causes of the war listed above are all geopolitical in nature. Although it was these factors that primarily influenced the government, many of the electorate supported U.S. efforts on the basis that this would preserve freedom and democracy for the South Vietnamese and save them from a Communist dictatorship. This was a truly altruistic attitude. The problem with this view was that the South Vietnamese leaders supported by the United States were not only corrupt, but did not practice democracy. Further, there was no thirst among the South Vietnamese peasantry for a U.S. style capitalistic democracy. What the North Vietnamese could offer as a vision was a united Vietnam (under their rule) and freedom from foreign domination. To many, perhaps most, Vietnamese, the United States represented a continuation of foreign domination.

Provocative Action by the North Vietnamese

What finally drew the United States irrevocably into the war was the perception that our armed forces were under attack by the North Vietnamese. In July 1964, the U.S. Navy ordered the destroyer *Maddox* to the Tonkin Gulf off North Vietnam to use a variety of electronic devices for eavesdropping and to determine the locations and frequency of enemy radars. The Communist Vietnamese had never officially defined their territorial waters, although Communist China maintained a twelve-mile limit. The *Maddox* was told to approach within eight miles of the coast and four miles of the offshore islands. Meanwhile, South Vietnamese commandos were conducting nightly raids on North Vietnamese facilities. On August 2, when the *Maddox* was about ten miles off the Red River delta, near an island attacked by the South Vietnamese two nights previously, the ship was fired upon by three Communist patrol boats. The *Maddox* radioed for help, and four jet planes from the aircraft carrier *Ticonderoga* arrived shortly thereafter. The planes sank one patrol boat and crippled the others. Only a single North Vietnamese machine gun round had hit the *Maddox*, and there were no casualties.

President Lyndon Johnson, who was in the midst of an election campaign, was informed of the military action and initially decided to play down the incident. However, the Navy decided to supersede the electronic monitoring with maneuvers designed to assert the right of freedom of the seas. The Navy also made contingency plans for reprisals in case of another attack. On the night of August 3, 1964, the *Maddox* and a companion destroyer, the *C. Turner Joy*, believed from radio and sonar signals that they were again under attack. Subsequent investigation has led to the conclusion that there was no second attack, but the President decided that firm action was called for, and he activated the contingency plans, leading to the first U.S. bombing missions against the North Vietnamese.[18] On August 5, the President sent Congress the following resolution for approval:

> Resolved by the Senate and House of Representatives of the United States of America in Congress assembled, That the Congress approves and supports the determination of the President, as Commander in Chief, to take all necessary measures to repel any armed attack against the forces of the United States and to prevent further aggression.[19]

The resolution was passed unanimously in the House and with only Senators Wayne Morse and Ernest Gruening opposing in the Senate. There followed further bombings of North Vietnamese installations. The marines were introduced into South Vietnam in March 1965. By the end of 1966, there were 267,000 U.S. ground forces in Vietnam, compared with 275,000 regular South Vietnamese troops and an estimated 101,000 men in the regular North Vietnamese army, which was supplemented by 170,000 irregulars. The United States was involved in a full-scale war. By March 1969, the United States deployed strength peaked at 625,866.

OUTCOME OF THE WAR

The Vietnamese War ended in complete defeat of the United States and South Vietnamese forces. The last Americans were evacuated from Saigon by helicopter on April 29, 1975, and the North Vietnamese forces entered the city the following day.

The official U.S. casualty figures from the war were 46,226 battle deaths and 10,326 other deaths for a total of 56,552. The wounded numbered 155,311. Approximately 2,700,000 men and women fought in the war, leaving many with deep psychological problems that resulted in difficulties ranging from drug abuse to involvement in violent crime. The estimated cost of the war was more than $150 billion, excluding interest on the debt and veterans and other benefits. This figure also excludes aid to the French before the Geneva agreements.

The war devastated Vietnam in both the north and south. In spite of complaints that the United States was fighting "with one arm tied behind its back," the total tonnage of bombs dropped by the United States on Vietnam and Cambodia during the conflict was three times that dropped on both Europe and Asia during all of World War II.[20] Not only did bombing destroy the infrastructure of roads and railways but the use of defoliants damaged much agricultural land. The war was responsible for the deaths of more than 1.5 million Vietnamese (185,000 South Vietnamese government soldiers, 924,000 North Vietnamese and South Vietnamese Communist soldiers, and 415,000 civilians).[21] The war also made refugees of 10 million South Vietnamese, about half of South Vietnam's total population. Any use of greater force would have literally destroyed South Vietnam in order to save it.

A side effect of the Vietnam War was the destabilization of neighboring Cambodia. The United States started bombing Cambodian territory in 1969 in an attempt to prevent its use as sanctuaries by North Vietnamese soldiers. This was followed by invasions by U.S. ground troops in 1970. The United States supported the government of Lon Nol, which was corrupt, even by Southeast Asia standards. The ineptitude and corruption of the Lon Nol forces, plus the dislocations caused by the bombing, were important factors in the eventual victory of the Khmer Rouge forces.[22]

Finally the war left the United States polarized into prowar and antiwar camps that it has taken a generation to heal. In fact, even in 1992, nearly twenty years after the end of the war, the actions that Governor Bill Clinton took to avoid military service in Vietnam were a major issue in the Presidential campaign.

PROBABLY UNNECESSARY WARS

WHAT IF THE UNITED STATES HAD NOT SUPPORTED SOUTH VIETNAM?

Following the Geneva Conference in 1954, the French essentially turned over responsibility for South Vietnam to the United States. The United States willingly accepted this role and helped its chosen leader, Ngo Dinh Diem, sabotage the Geneva agreement to hold supervised elections. If the United States had joined instead with France and Britain in demanding that these elections be held on schedule in 1956, the subsequent U.S. involvement probably would not have occurred. It is likely that the Communist side would have won the elections in both north and south. Further, its military power was such that it could have quickly put down any attempt by Diem to nullify the elections by force. If the United States had participated in arranging the elections, it could not very well have aided the South Vietnamese in any revolt.

Thus, without our involvement, Vietnam would have become a Communist state in 1956 instead of in 1975. However, it would have been a state with an infrastructure, industrial capacity, and agricultural potential that would have allowed it to develop in a far different way from its devastated state in 1975.

Moreover, in retrospect, whether Vietnam was in the Communist camp or allied with the West probably would not have significantly affected the global balance of power. It is obvious now that the seamless alliance of Communist states that was one reason for our entry into Vietnam never really existed. China and the Soviet Union split apart in 1962. Further, although China supported North Vietnam during the war, relations between the two countries quickly cooled once the Americans left. There had been an historical antipathy between the Vietnamese and Chinese people that both having Communist governments did not erase. There has been a small-scale border war between the two nations since the early 1980s.

We also know now that it is probable that the so-called domino effect would not have occurred in 1956 any more than it did in 1975. The remaining two parts of the former French Indochina, Laos and Cambodia, did become Communist states, but the predicted further fall of Thailand, Malaysia, Indonesia, and the Philippines never was threatened.

Finally, if the United States had not been involved in Vietnam, the tragic divisions in our own country would have been avoided. President Lyndon Johnson would have been able to pursue his War on Poverty without the inflationary and distracting influences of the Vietnam conflict, with probable salutary effects both on race relations and American economic development.

WAS THIS WAR NECESSARY?

The United States became involved in Vietnam to replace the French in the struggle to prevent the Communist North Vietnamese from extending their domination to South Vietnam. In this, we also sought to prevent the fall of Laos and Cambodia through the domino effect. The Vietnam War failed to achieve any of the aims that led to U.S. involvement. Accordingly, it comes under the first of the three categories of unnecessary wars established in the Introduction.

In fact, if one generalizes the aims that led us into the war as "improving the U.S. position in the world vis-a-vis the Communist nations," the war was counterproductive. The inflation caused by the war, the diversion of funds from domestic programs to armaments, and the social unrest arising from differing views of the war all left the United States an economically weaker nation in 1975 than it would have been if there had been no war.

Unlike the War of 1812 and the Spanish-American War, domestic politics had little to do with our entry into Vietnam, though everything to do with our eventual withdrawal. Nor was U.S. involvement traceable to a weak President unable to resist the pressure of the hawks. In spite of their faults, neither Presidents Kennedy nor Johnson could be considered weak leaders. However, they and most of their advisers suffered from the delusion that there was a monolithic Communist empire that had to be stopped each time it attempted to extend its influence by force. Memories of appeasement of Germany before World War II by not resisting Hitler's aggressive actions in Austria and Czechoslovakia colored the leaders' views of Communist actions in the 1960s. If Presidents Kennedy and Johnson had viewed the conflict between North and South Vietnam as a civil war in a remote part of the world that had little bearing on the U.S. national interest, they would undoubtedly have agreed that U.S. involvement was unwise and unnecessary.

POSSIBLY

UNNECESSARY

WARS

Chapter V

THE AMERICAN REVOLUTION

*I*n the cases of the three wars covered in the previous section, a number of reputable historians share the view presented in this book that these conflicts were probably unnecessary. However, there is no such consensus on the two wars in this section. Both the American Revolution and the Civil War had profound effects on the subsequent development of the country. Thus, any speculation on what might have happened if they had not taken place is on much shakier grounds. Accordingly, in this chapter, after examining the causes and effects of the American Revolution, we shall examine the history and present conditions of three other countries that were also former British colonies —Canada, Australia, and New Zealand—but did not revolt against the mother country. The chapter will conclude by examining the present differences between these revolutionary and nonrevolutionary nations.

HISTORICAL BACKGROUND

The first Charter of Virginia, granted by King James I on April 10, 1606, contained the following declaration:

> All and every the Persons, being our Subjects, which shall dwell and inhabit within every or any of the said several Colonies....shall have and enjoy all Liberties, Franchises, and Immunities....as if they had been

abiding and born within this our Realm of England, or any other of our said Dominions.[1]

To the colonists, these liberties included not only a fair trial and judgment by one's peers but also participation in their local government. The colonial assemblies passed laws, levied taxes, and raised troops for their own defense, functioning much as Parliament in England. Since the colonial charters had been granted by the king, the colonists tended to look to him, rather than to parliament. However, following the Glorious Revolution in 1688, the parliament grew progressively stronger in relation to the king. By the mid-1700s, parliament was attempting to govern the colonies directly, imposing both regulations on trade and levying taxes. When in March 1765, parliament passed the Stamp Act providing that all official documents be validated with a stamp provided by the British government, there were protest riots in every New England colony. This was "taxation without representation." The English heeded the protests, and the Stamp Act was repealed the following year. Following the repeal, there was general rejoicing. John Adams wrote six months later, "The repeal of the Stamp Act has composed every wave of popular disorder into a smooth and peaceful calm."[2]

However, the calm did not last. In 1767 Parliament passed the Townshend Acts, named after the Chancellor of the Exchequer who proposed them. These provided for duties on tea, glass, lead, paper, and painter's colors imported into the colonies. Again, there were furious protests, and Parliament repealed the Townshend Acts, with the exception of a minor tax of three pence a pound on tea. To minimize the effect of the tea tax, the East India Company was allowed to sell its tea to the colonists with a duty drawback on the normally heavy British duty. The effect was that the net price, including the detested tea tax of three pence a pound, was lower than competitive tea smuggled in from Holland.[3] The colonists, nevertheless, refused on principle to pay the tax on tea. In Philadelphia and New York City, ships containing tea were not allowed to land. In Boston, the tea ships landed, but a committee of prominent citizens disguised as Indians dumped the tea in the harbor, an event subsequently known as the Boston Tea Party. The outraged king and Parliament then passed a series of acts to punish the Bostonians. The port of Boston was closed until the destroyed tea was paid for; town meetings were forbidden without the governor's permission; and public buildings designated by the governor were to be used for the quartering of troops.[4]

There was general resentment in all of the colonies of these Intolerable Acts and, at the suggestion of Virginia, the First Continental Congress convened in Philadelphia in September 1774. The congress respectfully petitioned the king to put an end to the actions of Parliament in infringing upon their rights and urged a boycott of British trade until the despised legislation was repealed. The Congress also considered a plan proposed by James Galloway of Pennsylvania, which, if accepted by Britain, would have given the colonies self-rule in a sort of dominion status. It was defeated by one vote.[5] Before the Second Continental Congress scheduled for the following May, shots were exchanged between the Massachusetts colonial militia and the British regulars at the Battles of Lexington and Concord on April 19, 1775. The American Revolution had begun.

ECONOMIC FACTORS LEADING TO PRESSURES FOR WAR

A strong case for the economic causes of the American Revolution was made by the historian Louis M. Hacker in his book *The Triumph of American Capitalism.*[6] He stated that "In a functioning imperial economy, the capitalist relationships between mother country and colonies as a rule lead to a colonial unfavorable balance of payments." The southern colonies produced tobacco in return for goods and services needed on the plantations; the British invested their surplus in this exchange in southern agricultural operations. The northern colonies also imported from Britain more than they sold to it and attempted to earn the difference through trade, particularly the triangular trade in sugar, rum, and slaves. When non-British producers of sugar in the Caribbean undercut British prices, Britain attempted to prevent its importation into the colonies. Conflicting economic interests also developed in the South when the British monopolized the sale of real estate west of the Allegheny Mountains. With the British mercantile system automatically leading to an unfavorable balance of payments and with British legislation making it impossible for the Americans to develop compensating income, conflict was inevitable.

Other historians do not agree with this interpretation. Charles M. Andrews in *The Colonial Period of American History* holds that the Stamp Act and the Townshend Acts were passed with the aim of raising sorely needed revenue, rather than to help British merchants. Andrews admits that commercial and economic factors were initially important in the rise of the American effort to obtain self-government. However, in the end these economic and commercial factors were less important than the philosophical and political struggle for human rights and liberties.[7]

THE ROLE OF RADICALS

In the period leading up to the American Revolution, a number of patriots, including Thomas Paine, Patrick Henry, and Samuel Adams wrote and preached about the desirability of separation from Britain. In the terminology of this book, all three men were war hawks. All three were influential, but Samuel Adams was especially important in keeping the populace stirred up.[8]

While at Harvard College, Samuel Adams in 1743 wrote a thesis on the subject of "Whether it be lawful to resist the Supreme Magistrate, if the Commonwealth cannot otherwise be preserved." His affirmative answer to this question remained unwavering during the next thirty-five years. He eventually became clerk of the Massachusetts colonial assembly, and was elected to the Boston seat in the assembly in 1764. He had become so influential that he was chosen to write Boston's protest against the proposed Stamp Act, and he subsequently worked to secure its repeal. In 1765, the Massachusetts Colony's lieutenant governor, Thomas Hutchinson, wrote to England about Adams that "There is not a greater incendiary in the King's domain, or a man....who less scruples any measure however criminal to accomplish his purpose."

However, it was not fire but water that Samuel Adams used in his most famous escapade, the Boston Tea Party, which he organized. Although Philadelphia and New York City refused to let the British ships containing the taxed tea land, three ships did land in Boston. When the governor would not issue clearance papers for the vessels to return to Britain without unloading, Adams, who was chairman of the meeting discussing the problem, declared, "This meeting can do nothing more to save the country." Those attending the meeting then disguised themselves as Indians and dumped 342 chests of tea in the waters of Boston Harbor. The British now had a monetary grievance, and Parliament passed what became known as The Intolerable Acts to punish Boston. This set in motion the series of events culminating in the shots fired at Lexington on April 19, 1775. Adams, who heard the shots while on his way to Lexington with John Hancock, is reported to have remarked, "What a glorious morning for America!"

Samuel Adams' counterpart in Virginia was Patrick Henry. Born in 1736 in east-central Virginia, Henry left school at age fifteen. After two failing ventures as a storekeeper and one as a farmer, he turned to the law and was admitted to the bar after less than a month of study. His ability as a speaker made him popular in disputes that went to trial, and he handled 1,185 cases in his first three years of law practice. He was elected to the Virginia House of Burgesses in 1765, shortly after the passage of the Stamp Act. He made a fiery speech against the act, concluding with the words, "If this be treason, make the most of it!" Even better known is the peroration to his speech to the House of Burgesses in March 1775: "Is life so dear or peace so sweet as to be purchased at the price of chains and slavery? Forbid it, Almighty God! I know not what course others may take, but as for me, give me liberty or give me death." Although he briefly served as commander of the Virginia troops, the Committee of Public Safety, which supervised the troops, decided that Henry had greater talents as an agitator than as a military leader and persuaded him to resign his commission. After the war, he bitterly opposed the adoption of the Constitution on the basis that the proposed national government infringed on the rights of the states.

ANTIWAR SENTIMENT

Not all of the colonists supported the revolt. Many agreed with the Massachusetts lawyer who said it was a "causeless, wanton, wicked rebellion."[9] According to the patriot John Adams, throughout the war one third of the population was opposed to the war, one third was neutral, and only one third actively supported the conflict. Benjamin Franklin in March 1775 declared that "he had never heard in any conversation from any person drunk or sober the least expression of a wish for a separation or hint that such a thing would be advantageous for America." Even George Washington pledged to the New York Provincial Congress in 1776 that he would work for "harmony between the Mother Country and these Colonies."[10] Many of the loyalists, as the supporters of the king were known, left the country. More than 60,000 went to Upper Canada present-day Ontario) and the Maritime Provinces, with thousands more settling in the

West Indies or Britain.11 However, particularly after the doves left the country, the hawks obviously were in control.

RESULTS OF THE WAR

The American Revolution effectively ended with complete victory for the colonists on October 19, 1781, when Lord Cornwallis surrendered to General George Washington at Yorktown, Virginia. However, peace negotiations dragged on until 1783. The American negotiators, Benjamin Franklin, John Adams, and John Jay, eventually reached an agreement that gave the Americans all the land between the Alleghenies and the Mississippi, as well as substantial fishing rights off the Canadian coast.

The cost of the war was approximately $100 million, excluding interest on the debt and veterans' benefits. Officially, the American battle deaths were 4,435. There were undoubtedly additional war-related deaths, but these were not recorded.

Among the many results of the war was the confiscation of a number of large Loyalist estates and distribution of the land as small farms. The British inheritance systems of primogeniture and entail were abolished as well. The democratic aims of the Revolution were also achieved, as governors were chosen by the people, and the upper chambers of the legislatures were made elective instead of appointive.[9]

Apart from those farmers who benefitted from the breakup of the large confiscated estates, the day-to-day life of the average American probably was little changed by the Revolution. America in the 1780s was largely an agricultural society, with the farms self-sufficient to an extent almost unimaginable today, so the fact that taxes flowed to New York City (then the capitol) rather than to London had little practical effect.

POSSIBLY UNNECESSARY WARS

OTHER COLONIAL EXPERIENCES

At this point in previous chapters, we have asked the question "What if this war had not taken place?" However, as pointed out in the introductory paragraph, the American Revolution had such profound effects on subsequent American history that it would be difficult, or impossible, to construct a detailed alternate scenario. Therefore, we shall instead examine the history and present conditions of three other British colonies—Canada, Australia, and New Zealand—where the eventual separation from the mother country was peaceful, rather than revolutionary.

1. CANADA

The original settlers of Canada were French, but Britain gained control following the French and Indian war. Under the Treaty of Paris in 1763 which ended this war, France ceded to Britain the territory of Canada, as well as giving up other claims. Subsequently, the English-speaking colonists, originally outnumbered by the French, were substantially augmented by United Empire Loyalists who fled the American Revolution.

In 1791 Britain granted the Canadians, both English and French, the right to have popular assemblies with democratically elected representatives. Although these assemblies initially had relatively few powers, they gradually assumed important roles. In 1859, Canada started imposing tariffs on imported British goods and in 1862 assumed the burden of its own defense, as British troops were withdrawn. In 1867, the British North American Act was passed by the British Parliament. This act established the Dominion of Canada, uniting Nova Scotia, New Brunswick, Quebec, and Ontario. The new dominion purchased the territories controlled by the Hudson's Bay Company in 1869. These territories eventually became the provinces of Manitoba, Saskatchewan, and Alberta. Although the 1867 act granted Canada complete internal sovereignty, the responsibility for external defense and foreign affairs was initially retained by the Crown. These external responsibilities too were gradually ceded to Canada. In 1908, Canada acted to control immigrants from the British Isles. At the time of World War I, Canada asserted its independence by denying Britain's right to requisition Canadian ships. Since then, Canada has, in essence, been an independent nation with its own treaty-making powers and its own ambassadors to foreign countries. (The first ambassador to the United States, Vincent Massey, was appointed in 1926.)

The Canadian governmental system at the national level is modeled after the British. The Canadian Parliament is composed of two houses -- a Senate which, like the House of Lords in Britain, is appointed, not elected, and a House of Commons. Although there is a figurehead governor-general, appointed by the Crown, this office is largely ceremonial. Executive power is exercised by the prime minister, who must be a member of Parliament and must command the confidence of a majority of the members of the House of Commons. Unlike the United States, where the executive branch is independent of the legislative branch, the prime minister is directly responsible to the legislature. The prime minister not only chooses the heads of the government departments but also largely directs the making of laws, since his or her party controls the legislature. All powers not expressly granted to the provinces are reserved by the federal government. In addition to the national government, each of the Canadian provinces, which roughly correspond to the American states, has its own government. With the exception of Quebec, the provinces have only a single legislative body, whose members are directly elected. Each provincial government is headed by a premier who, with the provincial cabinet, is directly responsible to the provincial legislature.[13]

POSSIBLY UNNECESSARY WARS

2, AUSTRALIA

Although Australia was discovered by the Spaniard Luis de Torres in 1605, it was claimed for England in 1770 by Captain James Cook, who planted the British flag on Cape York, the northernmost point of the continent. Beginning in 1788, Britain started sending convicts to Australia, and other immigrants followed. Eventually, there were six colonial states, and a movement toward federation started in the last half of the nineteenth century. After much bickering between the states, the Commonwealth of Australia was authorized by the British Parliament and came into existence on January 1, 1901. Its constitution was modeled after that of the United States. Unlike Canada, all powers not specifically delegated to the federal government are retained by the states. Australia has generally been a pioneer in social legislation, establishing old age and invalid pensions in 1908 and a maternity allowance in 1912. Women's suffrage was granted in 1902, eighteen years before it was granted in the United States. Britain maintained nominal control over Australia's foreign relations until 1942, when it officially gained complete autonomy in both internal and external affairs.

As in the case of Canada, Australia now is essentially free and independent. There still is a governor-general, representing the Crown, but he is only a ceremonial figure. Australia has a bicameral Parliament, with a Senate and a House of Representatives. The members of both are directly elected. General elections are held at least once every three years. The prime minister and his cabinet must be elected members of Parliament. They represent the majority party in the House of Representatives. Each state also has a bicameral legislature and is headed by a premier.[14]

3. NEW ZEALAND

New Zealand's coastline, like Australia's, was explored in the late 1700s by the English explorer Captain James Cook. In 1840, the territory was annexed by Britain, and a treaty was executed with the Maori tribes, who recognized British sovereignty. However, there were continued wars with the Maoris until about 1870. In 1852, the British Parliament approved an act giving New Zealand representative government. It was declared a dominion in 1907 and obtained full autonomy in 1942, at the same time as Australia.

Although New Zealand originally was divided into provinces, these were abolished in 1870. There is a unicameral legislature, of whom four members by law are Maoris. The prime minister is the leader of the party holding the majority of seats in Parliament. The prime minister and his twenty-member cabinet exercise executive authority. Local government is based on county, municipality, and district. Women's suffrage was granted in 1893, twenty-seven years before it was enacted in the United States.[15]

POSSIBLY UNNECESSARY WARS

4. COMPARISONS
The following table compares some statistical and other measures for the four countries:

COMPARISONS BETWEEN U.S., CANADA, AUSTRALIA, AND N.Z.

Country/ Statistic	Canada	Austra- lia	N.Z.	United States
Form of Government	Parl- iament	Parl- iament	Parl- iament	Repub- lic
Literacy Rate	96%	89%	100%	96%
GNP per Cap.	$21M	$18M	$11M	$21M
Homicides per 100,000	6.3	3.4	2.5	7.9
Infant Mort- ality/1000	7.7	9.0	10.8	10.0
Life Expect- ancy (M/F)	73/80	73/79	71/77	73/80
Health Care	Public	Public	Public	Priv.
Newspaper Circ./Capita	211	308	324	259
System of Measure	Metric	Metric	Metric	Eng- lish

Sources:
1. *Countries of the World Yearbook, 1992* (Detroit: Gale Research).
2. Kurian, George, *The New Book of World Rankings* (New York: Facts on File, 1991).

Overall, the United States does not seem to have derived a significant advantage over the other three countries by having won its freedom by revolution. In fact, the

United States seems to have been less willing to adopt new ideas than the nonrevolutionary countries. All three other countries gave women the right to vote before the United States did. All three other countries have adopted the metric system of measurement, whereas the United States has stayed with the English system. The United States is the only country of the four that does not have a national system of health care.

WAS THIS WAR NECESSARY?

Based on these comparisons, I think a case can be made that the United States in the long run did not come out any better by having had a violent revolution. Was there any possibility that the differences leading up to the conflict could have been resolved peacefully? Certainly, Britain yielded to the pressure from the colonists in repealing the Stamp Act and all of the Townshend Act duties except the one on tea, which posed no economic penalty. Even after the Boston Tea Party and the Intolerable Acts of Parliament, the plan offered by James Galloway to the First Continental Congress, which failed of passage by one vote, offered the chance of a peaceful solution. Without the agitation of such men as Samuel Adams and Patrick Henry and with a different cast of characters on the British side, there might have been no war.

One can take the position that without the American revolutionary precedent, Canada, Australia, and New Zealand would not have been able to break away from Britain in a nonviolent manner. Maybe, but it seems very possible that by the time those colonies requested and received independence, the American Revolution was not a significant factor in Britain's willingness to let them go.

One can also argue that the American Revolution and subsequent adoption of the Constitution established a form of government that served as a model for all the later democracies. However, I believe that it is more likely that democracy was an idea whose time had come, and that France, Britain, and the other great Western nations would have chosen the democratic form of government they now have without the American model.

Of course, the United States today would be a very different nation if we had severed our ties with Great Britain in the twentieth century, as Canada did, rather than in the eighteenth century. As the comparative table shows, we might not be any "better," but we certainly would be different. There is no way of knowing for sure how our nation would have developed without the revolution, but I think it is at least possible that the American Revolution was an unnecessary war.

Chapter VI

THE CIVIL WAR

*T*his chapter on the Civil War will follow the same pattern as the previous chapter on the American Revolution. After background sections on slavery, the movement for secession, and a summary of the effects of the war, the chapter will examine the experience of other nations in coping with attempted secession.

SLAVERY AND POLITICS

The first twenty black slaves were brought by a Dutch vessel from the West Indies to the colony of Jamestown in Virginia in 1619. During the balance of the seventeenth century, about 25,000 more blacks were brought in to serve as household servants in the North and as agricultural laborers in the South. The slave traffic formed an integral part of the triangular trade in which New England rum was taken to Africa to exchange for slaves, the slaves were taken to the West Indies to exchange for sugar and molasses, which was brought to New England to make more rum. The slave trade was so profitable to the British that when the colonial legislature in Virginia passed bills forbidding further importation of slaves, the laws were vetoed by the king.

At the end of the seventeenth century, all the colonial legislatures still recognized slavery as legal, and there was only scattered individual protest against it. During the eighteenth century, there was a large influx of slaves, primarily to work on the plantations in the South. Some enlightened southerners deplored slavery, but no planter could afford to pay wages to free workers while his neighbor used slaves. By 1715, slaves constituted 25 percent of the population south of the Potomac River, as compared with less than 3 percent in New England. In the North, moral arguments against slavery prevailed, and by the end of the century every state north of Maryland except New Jersey had enacted laws that abolished slavery either immediately or gradually. The Northwest Ordinance, passed by the Continental Congress on July 13, 1787, provided that "There shall be neither slavery nor involuntary servitude in said territory," which included all the new territory between the Ohio River and the Great Lakes east to the Mississippi.[2] At the Constitutional convention held the same year that the Northwest Ordinance was passed, it was agreed that the slave trade would be phased out over a period of twenty years and that in the census used to determine a state's representation in Congress, blacks would be counted as three-fifths of a person.

With the exception of a law in 1808 codifying the Constitutional provision against further importation of slaves after that date, all of the congressional legislation during the first thirty years of our nation that touched on slavery essentially endorsed the continuation of that institution. Kentucky was admitted in 1792 with a constitution that sanctioned slavery. The fugitive slave law of 1793 allowed a slave owner to reclaim a runaway slave in any state through the decision of a local judge, without a jury trial. When the territory of Mississippi was organized in 1798, slavery was permitted. In 1805 a bill in congress to emancipate the slaves in the District of Columbia was decisively defeated. However, when the territory of Missouri applied for admission in 1818 with a constitution that authorized slavery, there was considerable opposition from northern congressmen. Missouri was significant in that it was to be the first new state west of the Mississippi to be added to the existing twenty-two states, eleven of which permitted slavery and eleven which did not. The impasse was broken when Maine (which had been part of Massachusetts) also applied for admission. The Missouri Compromise of 1820 admitted both, along with a proviso that prohibited slavery in all of the Louisiana Purchase territory north of the latitude of the southern boundary of Missouri (excepting Missouri itself).[3]

The westward expansion continued, and between 1843 and 1846 the United States annexed Texas, took California and New Mexico from Mexico, and signed a treaty with Britain for the Oregon territory up to the 49th parallel. The question of the status of slavery in the new territories became paramount. Under the Compromise of 1850 proposed by Henry Clay, California was admitted as a free state; the rest of the territories ceded by Mexico was divided into New Mexico and Utah; slave trade (but not slavery) was prohibited in the District of Columbia; and a stricter fugitive slave law was enacted. Among other provisions of the fugitive slave law, the fugitive was not allowed a trial, and any citizen who aided the fugitive was subject to a thousand dollar fine.[4] Hundreds of mass meetings were held in the North to protest the onerous provisions of this act. Mass meetings were also held four years later to protest the passage by Congress of the Kansas-Nebraska Act, which nullified the Missouri Compromise and left the question of slavery up to the inhabitants of the new territories. One result was the formation of a new Republican party in July 1854. Started as a state party in Michigan, it became a national party in 1856. In 1857, Chief Justice Roger B. Taney and a majority of the Supreme Court declared in the Dred Scott case that Congress had no power to exclude slavery from the territories. The following year, a former Illinois congressman named Abraham Lincoln was nominated as the Republican candidate for senator from Illinois. In a series of debates with the Democratic officeholder, Stephen A. Douglas, on whether slavery in the territories should be controlled by Congress or by popular vote of the people in the territory, Lincoln opposed the Dred Scott decision (that it was unconstitutional for Congress to forbid slavery in the territories) and held that the question of slavery in the territories <u>should</u> be decided by Congress. Douglas defended popular sovereignty, which he interpreted as including the right of the people of a territory to exclude slavery. Douglas won the election by a narrow margin.

In the Presidential election of 1860, the Democrats split into two wings. The "regulars" nominated Douglas. The proslavery wing of the party was unhappy over Douglas's position that the territories could exclude slavery and nominated John C. Breckenridge. The Republicans nominated Abraham Lincoln on the third ballot. Although in the ensuing election Lincoln received less than half of the popular votes, he received 180 electoral votes, compared with 123 for his opponents.

SECESSION

Senator John C. Calhoun of South Carolina in his last speech to the Senate, read on March 4, 1850, made an impassioned plea to his fellow senators to cease agitation on the slave question and to amend the Constitution to "restore to the South, in substance, the power she possessed of protecting herself, before the equilibrium between the sections was destroyed by the action of this Government." He went on to say:

> We, as representatives of the States of this Union, ...should come to a distinct understanding of our respective views, in order to ascertain whether the great questions at issue can be settled or not. If you, who represent the stronger portion, cannot agree to

settle them on the basis of justice and duty, say so; and let the States we both represent agree to separate and part in peace. If you are unwilling we should part in peace, tell us so, and we shall know what to do, when you reduce the question to submission or resistance. If you remain silent, you will compel us to infer by your actions what you intend. In that case, California will become the test case. If you admit her,....we would be blind not to perceive that your real objects are power and aggrandizement, and infatuated not to act accordingly.[5]

During the next ten years, many of the elite in the South became increasingly concerned with the actions of the abolitionists in the north. Rather than arguing as they had in the past that slavery was an inherited evil that would soon pass away, southerners now claimed that slavery was a positive good, that it should be made permanent, and that it should be allowed throughout the United States.[6] The historian Lee Benson states that the conflicting views of the northern abolitionists and southern secessionists on the issue of slavery escalated into a conflict "over the rights, principles, honor, and self-esteem of Northern and Southern *white citizens*."[7] Southern fears increased after John Brown led a raid on the government armory at Harper's Ferry, Virginia, to secure weapons to liberate and arm the slaves. Although the armory was soon retaken by a detachment of marines and John Brown was captured and executed, the response of many abolitionists that he was a martyr convinced many in the South that this was the beginning of a movement that would destroy their way of life.

The secessionist movement gained strength during the Presidential campaign of 1860. Even before the campaign started, one of the secessionist leaders, A.B. Rhett, urged in a speech on July 4, 1859, in Grahamville, South Carolina, that the South demand the rights of slavery in all the territories or end the Union. William H. Yancey of Alabama said in a speech in Charleston, South Carolina, that same summer:

> We have eight million people educated in the use of arms, trained in self reliance, with a thorough knowledge of governmental principles, with as much real spirit and manhood as was ever possessed by any people....We have a great product without which the world cannot do.

Yancey went on to ask why eight million Southerners could not win freedom from the North when it took only three million Americans to win freedom from Britain.[8] It was this same Yancey who led the Alabama delegates out of the Democratic convention held in Charleston, South Carolina, in April 1860 after the convention adopted a platform without the southern plank stating that Congress must protect slavery in every part of the United States. The historian David Saville Muzzey states, "It was the defiant deed of men who were determined to listen to no further discussion of their demands for the recognition of slavery as a *right* -- a moral, social, and political right."[9] The delegates from Alabama who exited the convention were followed by those of five other southern states. The two wings of the Democratic party met again in Baltimore in June, with the northern wing nominating Stephen Douglas and the southerners John C. Breckenridge of Kentucky.

When the election of Abraham Lincoln as President was announced. the legislature of South Carolina was in session. It voted to call a convention to meet in December to consider the subject of secession. The convention met in Charleston and on December 20, 1860, voted unanimously that "the Union now subsisting between South Carolina and the other states, under the name of *United States of America*, is hereby dissolved."[10] Within six weeks of the secession of South Carolina, six other southern states had also severed themselves from the Union. In February 1861, representatives of these states met in Montgomery, Alabama, and organized the Confederate States of America, with Jefferson Davis as president. A constitution was drawn up that was similar to the United States Constitution except that slavery was expressly permitted, Congress was forbidden to levy protective tariffs, and the president was elected for a single six-year term. Rather surprisingly, the southern constitution contained a prohibition of "the importation of negroes of the African race from any foreign country."[11]

In President Abraham Lincoln's First Inaugural Address, delivered on March 4, 1861, he made an explicit attempt to reassure the South about the slavery issue. He quoted from one of his previous speeches to say:

> "I have no purpose, directly or indirectly, to interfere with the institution of slavery in the States where it exists. I believe I have no lawful right to do so, and I have no inclination to do so." I now reiterate these sentiments.

The speech also acknowledged the threat of secession and pleaded with the South not to take precipitate action. "Nothing can be lost by taking time... The government will not assail you. You can have no conflict without being yourselves the aggressors."[12]

At the time of the inauguration, all of the military property in the South formerly under the control of Washington had been seized by the secessionist government, with two exceptions—Fort Sumter in Charleston harbor and Fort Pickens in Florida. Actually, Fort Sumter had been vacant for a number of years before it was reoccupied by Union forces in December 1860, after South Carolina had seceded. The commander of Fort Sumter, Major Robert Anderson, requested supplies and reinforcement, but the first relief ship, sent the previous January, was fired upon and turned back. On March 29, Lincoln called a cabinet meeting to consider a memorandum from General Winfield Scott, the highest general in the army, recommending that both Fort Sumter and Fort Pickens be evacuated. However, the cabinet members, with the exception of William Seward and Caleb Smith, were in favor of reprovisioning Fort Sumter. Lincoln came to the conclusion that his oath of office demanded that he take a stand. Accordingly, on April 4, Lincoln sent a special messenger to the South Carolina governor to say that the fort would be supplied with provisions but that no soldiers or ammunition would be landed if there was no resistance. Before the relief expedition arrived, General Pierre Beauregard, Confederate commander in Charleston, demanded Fort Sumter be evacuated. When Major Anderson refused to comply, the first shell was fired by the Confederacy just before dawn on April 12, 1861. Major Anderson held out for two days but was forced to surrender.[13] The Civil War had commenced.

OTHER CAUSES OF THE CIVIL WAR

Not all historians agree that the institution of slavery was the main cause of the Civil War. Charles and Mary Beard make a strong case that a conflict between the static, agrarian South and the dynamic, industrializing North was inevitable. They and others believe that the moral indignation of the North over slavery was merely a cover for its desire to subjugate the South economically.[14] However, the economic theory of causation of the war does not seem to be accepted by most current historians.

There is also a group of historians termed "revisionist." Charles Ramsdell writes that by 1860 slavery had reached its peak and would have fallen by natural causes. In particular, none of the new territories that were the subject of dispute were suitable for crops like cotton which required slave labor. He points out that the census of 1860 showed only two slaves in all of Kansas. Even in the states where cotton was grown, Ramsdall postulates that overproduction and consequent low prices of cotton would have been reflected in the value of slaves, which would have become an increasingly unprofitable burden.[15] James G. Randall, sometimes also classified as a revisionist, makes a somewhat different point — that it was small minorities of irresponsible agitators on both sides that really led to the war. Randall argues that it was the abolitionists in the North and the secessionists in the South who through their fanaticism brought on the conflict.[16]

RESULTS OF THE WAR

The war ended with complete victory for the Union when General Robert E. Lee surrendered at Appomattox on April 9, 1865. Five days later, on the fourth anniversary of the surrender of Fort Sumter, President Lincoln was assassinated. His successor, President Andrew Johnson, appointed military governors of the states that had seceded, and the long process of reconstruction began.

The cost of the war was approximately $3 billion to the Union side and $1.5 billion to the Confederacy, excluding debt interest and veterans' benefits. The battle deaths on the two sides totaled more than 210,000; including war-related deaths from disease and accident, the total was more than 525,000.

The war achieved its aims of preserving the Union and liberating the slaves. The Thirteenth Amendment to the Constitution prohibited slavery and involuntary servitude. The Fourteenth Amendment guaranteed the civil rights of blacks and disqualified the leaders of the Confederacy from holding state or federal office. Ratification of this amendment was made a condition for the southern states to be readmitted to the Union.

With the Reconstruction Act of 1867, new governments were established under a provision that blacks not only were allowed to vote but should participate in running the new governments. The result, as described by historian David Saville Muzzey, was that "the rule of these governments of 1868 was an indescribable orgy of extravagance, fraud, and disgusting incompetence—a travesty on government."[17] Southerners responded by forming the Ku Klux Klan and other antiblack organizations. The resulting bitterness between the North and South lasted nearly a century.

FURTHER THOUGHTS ON SECESSION

Because of the irreconcilable positions of the northern Abolitionists and the Southern secessionists, it is unlikely that secession could have been prevented. However, secession did not automatically mean war. More than four months passed between the Mississippi resolution on secession on November 30, 1860, and the firing on Fort Sumter on April 12, 1861.

During that period, Horace Greeley, editor of the New York *Tribune* and one of the most influential men in the Republican party, wrote, "If the cotton states decide that they can do better out of the Union than in it, we insist on letting them go in peace....We hope never to live in a republic whereof one section is pinned to the other with bayonets."[18] Although the *Tribune* was a New York City newspaper, it had a national circulation. Greeley had consistently opposed slavery in the editorial columns of his newspaper, so his views carried weight, even with the abolitionists. However, Greeley was not an admirer of Abraham Lincoln, whose government he referred to as "demoralizing, disorganizing, and destructive,"[19] so his views probably had little effect on the President.

On the other hand, one of Lincoln's advisers, General Winfield Scott, the highest-ranking general in the Army, agreed with Greeley. Scott was a hero of both the War of 1812 and the Mexican-American war. He had been nominated for the Presidency by the Whigs in 1852. As a peacemaker, he had settled disputes between settlers of Maine and New Brunswick in the so-called Aroostook War boundary dispute, as well as arbitrating a similar dispute over the ownership of the island of San Juan in Puget Sound. In the face of possible war over secession, Scott advised letting "the wayward sisters depart in peace."

Obviously Abraham Lincoln did not agree with these views and was determined to preserve the Union.

Let us now examine some other cases where secession did <u>not</u> lead to civil war.

Czechoslovakia

Czechoslovakia was formed after World War I by uniting Bohemia (Cêchy in the Czech language), which had been dominated by Austria, and Slovakia, which had been dominated by Hungary. Both Bohemia and Slovakia are slavic lands with similar languages. Under its first president, Thomas Masaryk, the country prior to the Second World War was a thriving democracy. The Slovakia area remained more agricultural than Bohemia, which rapidly industrialized.

Czechoslovakia was occupied by the Soviet Union after the Second World War but was one of the first of the satellite nations to establish a democratic government following the breakdown of Soviet authority. Václev Havel, a poet and playwright, was elected president in 1989, after the so-called Velvet Revolution. In parliamentary elections for the assembly held in June 1992, nationalist parties in Slovakia and the Czech republic each received about 34 percent of the votes. In negotiating to form a government, they reached an impasse. The Czechs insisted on a federation recognized internationally as a single country; the Slovaks wanted a confederation of two independent states, each with international recognition. In an address to the assembly, Havel is reported to have said that if they ended up dismantling the country, they should do so in a way that would show the world what a civilized separation could be like.[20] Presumably, Havel could have called on the Czech army to prevent the secession of Slovakia but chose not to do so. On January 1, 1993, the two states became independent sovereign republics.

The Soviet Union

Mikhail Gorbachev was chosen by the Communist Party Central Committee to be General Secretary, the de facto head of state, when Konstantin Chernenko died in 1985. During his first years in office, Gorbachev initiated a number of reforms, including reduction of censorship and improvement in observance of human rights. In 1988, Gorbachev also assumed the position of Chairman of the Presidium, the titular head of state. In March 1989, elections were held for the new Congress of People's Deputies. These were the first contested elections since the earliest days of the Soviet Union, and the resulting congress conducted free and lively debates. The congress elected Gorbachev head of state with the title Chairman of the Supreme Soviet and chose from its own ranks the members of the legislature, the Supreme Soviet.

Among those winning seats in the March 1989 election was Boris Yeltsin. Yeltsin had been the Moscow party chief and a member of the Politburo until February 1988, when he was ousted by Gorbachev for pursuing a program of reform more radical than Gorbachev's. He won a landslide victory for the Moscow-wide seat in the March elections. He also was elected President of Parliament of the Russian Republic. During 1990, Gorbachev continued to press his policies of *perestroika* ("restructuring"), *glasnost* ("openness"), and democratization. However, as controls were eased, pressures built up in the republics to control more of their own affairs.

The first defiant actions came in the Baltic republics of Lithuania, Latvia, and Estonia, which had been forcibly annexed by the Soviet Union in June 1940. After Latvia and

Lithuania declared their independence in December 1990, armed Soviet commandos stepped in early in January 1991. They surrounded the main newspaper publishing plant in Latvia's capital, Riga, and the Communist headquarters in Lithuania's capital, Vilnius. On January 13, Soviet troops stormed the television broadcast center in Vilnius and thirteen people were killed. However, Russian president Boris Yeltsin pledged support of the Baltic republics, and both the United States and the European Community called for negotiation, rather than the use of force. The situation remained tense, but there was no further bloodshed.

Pressure from the other republics also continued, and Gorbachev negotiated a power-sharing arrangement with nine of the fifteen republics. Before the treaty was signed, a group of Communists seeking return of centralized authority undertook a coup d'etat on August 19, 1991, while President Gorbachev was on vacation. Boris Yeltsin defied the coup leaders, and the coup collapsed from lack of support by the populace and the military.

In the wake of the coup, the All-Soviet Congress on September 6, 1991, voted to turn over power to a new State Council, composed of Gorbachev and leaders of most of the republics. The following day, the State Council officially recognized the independence of the Baltic republics. However, the State Council was also short-lived. On December 22, 1991, all of the former Soviet republics except the Baltic states and Georgia agreed to be members of a new organization called the Commonwealth of Independent States.[21]

In essence, there were fifteen different secessions with almost no armed conflict (although ethnic conflict within some of the seceding states continues). If Gorbachev had taken the position that he had taken an oath of office to defend the Soviet Union and had used the power of the Soviet army and the KGB, there could well have been a number of civil wars. The terrible war resulting from the decision of the central government of Yugoslavia not to allow the secessions of Croatia and Bosnia-Herzgovinia shows what could have happened on a vastly larger scale in the former Soviet Union.

WAS THE AMERICAN CIVIL WAR NECESSARY?

As noted above, the strongly opposing views of the northern abolitionists and the southern secessionists made the secession of the southern states almost inevitable. However, civil war following secession was not inevitable. Had Abraham Lincoln listened to and acted on the advice of General Scott and Horace Greeley and given the southern states their freedom along with those Union properties located within their borders, including Fort Sumter, war probably could have been avoided. As noted above, Havel and Gorbachev avoided civil war in their countries by permitting secession.

On the other hand, even though the war began over the question of secession rather than that of slavery, one can take the position that war was necessary to free the slaves. However, this position, too, is arguable. Slavery had been abolished by law in 1833 in Great Britain and all of her colonies, including the West Indies. By 1860, slavery had been abolished throughout South and Central America (with the exception of Brazil, where it was abolished in 1889). It seems probable that the pressure of world opinion would have forced the South to emancipate the slaves within twenty years, even if the Confederacy had endured as a sovereign nation. Of course, for the slaves, twenty years would have been a long time, but even after their actual emancipation at the end of the Civil War in 1865, most of the former slaves endured poverty and racial persecution as free men that made their lives little better than they had been under slavery. Was it worth half a million lives to achieve this marginal improvement in their condition a few years earlier? I'm not sure.

WARS

UNNECESSARY

FOR THE AGGRESSOR

Chapter VII

THE FIRST WORLD WAR

*T*he three wars covered in this section, Wars Unnecessary for the Aggressor, fall under the first of the conditions mentioned in the introduction—they did not achieve the aims of the power that originated the conflict. Of course, once these wars started, it was necessary for the countries that had been attacked, along with their allies, to resist the aggressor. In all three cases—the First World War, the Second World War, and the Korean War—the aggressor eventually was defeated.

HISTORICAL BACKGROUND OF THE FIRST WORLD WAR

As this book is being written, Serbia is again in the headlines for its attacks on the breakaway republics of Bosnia-Herzgovinia and Croatia, which it wants to incorporate into a Greater Serbia. There once was a Greater Serbia, when in the fourteenth century the kingdom dominated the Balkans from the Danube to the Gulf of Corinth. In the fifteenth century, Serbia was conquered by Turkey and remained under Turkish rule until the nineteenth century, when the Congress of Berlin in 1878 granted it independence. In 1903, King Peter I ascended the Serbian throne after his supporters had hacked to death the previous king and queen and thrown their bodies out the palace window. King Peter's eldest son, Prince Djordje, was struck off the line of succession after he kicked his valet to death. On his accession to the throne, King Peter resolved to unite all the Serbs and restore Serbia to its golden age.[1] In the First Balkan War in 1912, Peter and his allies, Bulgaria, Greece, and Montenegro, decisively defeated the Turkish army. After the armistice that ended this war, Greece and Serbia agreed to split the former Turkish province of Macedonia between them. The following year, Serbia ganged up with Greece, Montenegro and Romania to attack Bulgaria in what was known as the Second Baltic War. They won a quick victory, and each took a piece of Bulgaria as their spoils. The Serbian prime minister then stated, "The first round is won. Now we must prepare for the second round, against Austria."[2] Austria-Hungary had a large Serbian minority population.

During the First and Second Balkan wars, the great powers in Europe had no direct involvement. However, both before and after these wars, the powers were busy negotiating alliances and building up their armies and navies. Russia formed an alliance with France that obliged both parties to move against Germany if either was attacked. Germany and Austria-Hungary also formed an alliance, which obliged Germany to support Austria in the event of a conflict with Russia. Both alliances courted Britain, but the French won out. The result was that the Triple Alliance of Germany, Austria, and Italy opposed the Triple Entente of France, Russia, and Britain. (Italy later defected to the other side.) These alliances did not make war inevitable, but they did guarantee that any conflict involving two of the great powers would lead to general war. The smaller countries sought protection from the great powers, with Serbia allied with Russia, and Belgium securing guarantees of her neutrality from France and Britain. Germany realized that an outbreak of war would mean fighting on two fronts against France and Russia. Count Alfred von Schlieffen, chief of the German General Staff, based his plans on a quick victory over the French after an attack through Belgium, followed by shifting his forces to the Russian front.[3]

In addition to forming alliances and making battle plans, several of the great powers believed that a war would allow them to realize long-term goals. Austria, in particular, felt threatened by the Serb minorities inside its border and by threats from the kingdom of Serbia, which it dearly wanted to defeat militarily. The French wished to recover the provinces of Alsace and Lorraine, which they had lost in the Franco-Prussian War. The Russians wanted to open the straits of the Dardanelles to give their Black Sea fleet access to the Mediterranean. In fact, some revisionist historians of the 1920s, such as Harry Elmer Barnes, blamed France and Russia, rather than Austria and Germany, for having orchestrated the events leading to war.[4] (This view is no longer widely accepted.)

In each of the courts, there were hawks and doves. In the Austrian court, the principle dove was the heir apparent, the Archduke Francis Ferdinand, while the principal hawk was General Conrad von Hotzendorf, head of the General Staff. In a letter to the foreign minister, Count Leopold von Berchtold, the Archduke wrote, "Don't let yourself be influenced by Conrad—ever! Naturally, he wants every possible war, every kind of hooray! rashness that will conquer Serbia and God knows what else.... Let's not play Balkan warriors ourselves....Let's stay aloof and watch the scum bash in each other's skulls." Berchtold agreed with the Archduke and at that time also sought a peaceful solution to the crisis.[5]

The event that all historians agree precipitated the war took place in Sarajevo, the capital of Bosnia. Bosnia had been under Austrian control since the defeat of the Turks in 1878 and was formally annexed by Austria in 1908. In 1914, three Bosnian youths of Serbian extraction decided to strike a blow for Bosnian independence. They made contact with a terrorist organization in Serbia called the Black Hand, which supplied them with arms and helped them smuggle these back into Bosnia. On June 28, 1914, one of the

WARS UNNECESSARY FOR THE AGGRESSOR

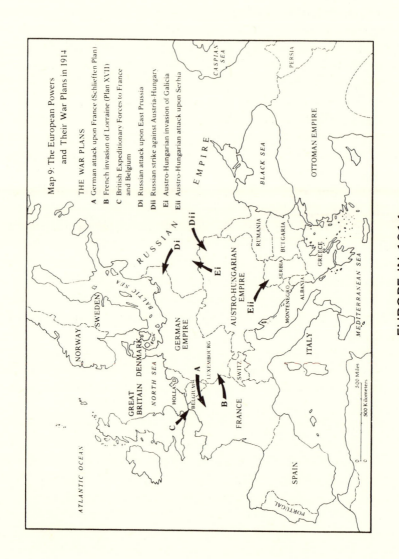

Map 9: The European Powers and Their War Plans in 1914

THE WAR PLANS

A German attack upon France (Schlieffen Plan)
B French invasion of Lorraine (Plan XVII)
C British Expeditionary Forces to France and Belgium
Di Russian attack upon East Prussia
Dii Russian strike against Austria-Hungary
Ei Austro-Hungarian invasion of Galicia
Eii Austro-Hungarian attack upon Serbia

EUROPE IN 1914

(From Paul Kennedy's *The Rise and Fall of thr Great Powers*) conspirators, Gavrilo Princip, took advantage of an opportunity during the visit of Archduke Francis Ferdinand to Sarajevo to observe military maneuvers to assassinate the archduke and his wife. The degree of complicity of the Serbian government in this act is in dispute, but at the very least, the Serbian prime minister, Nikola Pashich, had knowledge of the conspiracy and did not warn the Austrian government.[6] The historical irony is that Princip assassinated the one man in the Austrian court who was working to prevent an Austrian attack on Serbia.

Following the assassination, the Austrian foreign minister, Count von Berchtold, sent his chief assistant, Count Alexander Hoyos, to Berlin with a letter from Emperor Franz Joseph to Kaiser Wilhelm II that spoke of the need to "neutralize Serbia as a political power factor." Berchtold, who drafted the letter for the Emperor's signature, still hoped for a peaceful solution to this crisis and thought his letter would lead in this direction. Berchtold did not realize that Hoyos held rabidly anti-Serbian views. Hoyos told the Germans that the Austrian note really constituted a proposal to crush Serbia militarily and asked for the support of the Kaiser. This he received. Although the results were not what Berchtold had expected, he quickly adjusted his position and proposed that Austria issue an unacceptable ultimatum to Serbia, to be followed by invasion when it was rejected by the Serbs. The aged Franz Josef reluctantly agreed to the plan. However, Berchtold decided to deceive his opponents by having the Austrian minister of war and General von Hotzendorf both leave Vienna for vacations. The Kaiser and the German foreign minister also took vacations, as did the president of France and the British foreign secretary.

Then, while everybody was still on vacation, on July 23 Austria delivered to Serbia a "note" that amounted to an ultimatum including ten demands, of which the last was "the participation of Austrian Police in the suppression and apprehension of anti-Austrian subversive groups", and asked for a reply within forty-eight hours. Just after the expiration of the time limit, Serbia agreed to all demands except the last. This might have led to negotiation, but the Austrian government was intent on ending the perceived Serbian threat, both externally and internally. Accordingly, three days later, on July 28, 1914, Austria announced that the Serbian reply was unacceptable and declared war on Serbia.[7]

At this point, Russia ordered a general mobilization of its troops, although the Czar promised that his armies would not attack as long as negotiations continued. Alarmed by the Russian general mobilization, which was viewed as a prelude to attack, Germany ordered its own general mobilization on August 1 and declared war on Russia the same day. The Germans followed this with a declaration of war on France on August 3 and started to carry out the Schlieffen plan of invasion of France through Belgium. This violation of Belgian neutrality brought Britain into the war. The First World War had commenced.[8]

UNITED STATES ENTRY INTO THE FIRST WORLD WAR

During the first two years of the First World War the United States maintained a position of neutrality. Both sides courted the United States. The fact that English was a common language was of great value to Britain but, on the other hand, the Germans were the largest non-English minority and sympathized with their fatherland. Further, the British initially incensed the Americans by declaring a blockade not only of the enemy but also of any country known to be trading with the enemy. The United States objected vociferously that this violated the freedom of the seas. However, American anger at the British was overshadowed by American outrage at the Germans after they began their campaign of submarine warfare. The Cunard liner *Lusitania* was sunk off the coast of Ireland in May 1915, with 128 Americans among the 1,198 victims. After vehement American protests, the Germans promised not to sink passenger ships and to warn other ships before sinking them. As the war dragged on, though, the Germans decided that they would gain more from unrestricted submarine warfare than they would lose from U.S. intervention. After all, in 1916, the U.S. Army had only about 110,000 men, most of whom were occupied trying to chase Pancho Villa in Mexico. The U.S. armed forces had 55 airplanes, but no tanks. In short, the Germans expected U.S. intervention to have little effect on the outcome of the war, whereas they thought that unrestricted submarine warfare would give them a decisive victory.   President Woodrow Wilson was reelected to a second term in 1916 on the slogan "He kept us out of war!" However, before he was inaugurated for his second term, Germany issued its proclamation removing all past restrictions on its submarine warfare, except for allowing one plainly marked U.S. passenger ship a week to sail through a narrow lane to Britain. Not surprisingly, the German policy of unrestricted submarine warfare was unacceptable to the President, who broke off relations with Germany on February 3, 1917. However, he decided that there must be an unequivocal act of hostility by the Germans before he could declare war. In the middle of March, the Germans obliged by sinking four clearly marked American merchant ships, with a loss of thirty-six lives.

American public opinion had already been inflamed by Britain's release of a coded message from the German foreign secretary, Arthur Zimmerman, to the German ambassador in Mexico. It proposed that if Mexico sided with the Germans in the event that the United States entered the war, Germany would help Mexico recover Texas, New Mexico, and Arizona. The note also proposed that Germany would offer Japan pieces of the American West if Japan switched its allegiance from the Triple Entente to the Triple Alliance.[9]

Thus, the public was ripe for accepting Wilson's message to Congress on April 2, 1916, asking for a declaration of war. In it, he stated, "We have no quarrel with the German people, but only with the military despotism of Germany. The world must be made safe for democracy..." The declaration of war was passed by Congress on April 6, 1917.[10]

OUTCOME OF THE WAR

After being decisively defeated, the Germans on behalf of their allies signed an armistice agreement on November 11, 1918. At the ensuing peace conference held in Versailles, France, the Germans were excluded, and negotiations were held largely between President Woodrow Wilson of the United States, Prime Minister David Lloyd George of Great Britain, Premier Georges Clemenceau of France, and Premier Vittorio Orlando of Italy. Out of the conference came five treaties, one with each of the Central Powers.

The Treaty of Sèvres with Turkey dismantled the old Ottoman Empire. The Treaty of St. Germain-en-Laye and the Treaty of the Trianon with Hungary did the same for the Hapsburg Empire, establishing Yugoslavia and Czechoslovakia out of Serbia and parts of the former empire. The Treaty of Neuilly also took away parts of Bulgaria. Finally, the Treaty of Versailles imposed harsh conditions on Germany. It lost Alsace-Lorraine to France, the Sudetenland to Czechoslovakia, and a corridor to the North Sea to Poland. Germany agreed to pay large reparations and acknowledged its sole guilt and responsibility for the war. Germany objected to the treaty, but eventually signed it. However, the United States Senate then refused to ratify it. The Senate also refused to ratify the treaty establishing the League of Nations, even though President Wilson had agreed to water down some of its controversial provisions, such as freedom of the seas.

A very important, though indirect, result of the First World War was the triumph of Communism in Russia. By the end of 1916, the Russian army had suffered casualties of more than 3,600,000 dead and wounded. An additional 2,600,000 Russian soldiers had been captured. The decision in early 1917 to call up the second category of recruits, who were the sole breadwinners of their families, produced a wave of peasant unrest.[11] The February Revolution of that year forced the abdication of the Czar and the formation of a provisional government under Alexander Kerensky. To destabilize the provisional government, the Germans allowed the Bolshevik revolutionary V.I. Lenin, who had been in exile for eleven years, to transit Germany in a sealed railway car. Lenin was joined by Leon Trotsky and Josef Stalin. Although an offensive launched by Kerensky in July 1917 was initially successful against the Austrians, the Russian front collapsed under counterattacks from the Germans. In the so-called October Revolution, the Bolsheviks under Lenin and Trotsky seized power. The Revolution spread rapidly, and the Bolsheviks soon took Russia out of the war.[12] If there had been no war, there probably still would have been social upheaval in Russia, but the government might have ended up as social revolutionary, rather than Communist.

The casualties in the First World War were staggering. At least 8,600,000 men died. and more than 21,000,000 were wounded. Both French and German casualties amounted to about 70 percent of those mobilized, with the figure reaching 90 percent in Austria. The United States lost about 116,00 men, with another 234,000 wounded, a casualty rate of about 8 percent. The monetary cost of the war was well over $300 billion.[13]

For all its cost and horror, the First World War was not really decisive. Germany retained most of its industry, and now had a strong sense of grievance over the harsh terms of the Treaty of Versailles. The concept of the League of Nations, which sought to prevent future disagreements between nations from escalating into war, was never generally accepted. French Marshal Foch said when he read the Treaty of Versailles, "This isn't peace! This is a truce for twenty years!" He was tragically right, for the Second World War broke out twenty years and sixty-seven days after the Treaty of Versailles was signed.[14]

WAS THIS WAR NECESSARY FOR THE AGGRESSORS?

Although the assassination of Archduke Francis Ferdinand in Sarajevo on June 28, 1914, precipitated the series of events that led to the First World War, the progression from assassination to battle was not inevitable. Following the first flurry of outrage, the situation remained relatively calm for nearly a month. If Austria had not sent its ultimatum to Serbia on July 23, or if it had agreed to negotiate after Serbia's relatively conciliatory reply on July 25, the war might not have occurred.

The war that did take place achieved none of the aims of the aggressors. The Austrian-Hungarian Empire, far from subduing Serbia, ceased to exist. The Ottoman Empire also disappeared. Germany, rather than weakening the circle of antagonists surrounding it, lost territory to France, Czechoslovakia, and Poland. Thus, using the criteria established in the introductory chapter, this was an unnecessary war for the aggressors.

On the other hand, it became a necessary war for France, Britain, and Russia and eventually, for the United States. The Germans made a serious miscalculation when they decided that the benefits of unrestricted submarine warfare exceeded the liability of U.S. entry into the war. The financial strength, the industrial might, and the manpower of the United States provided the decisive edge to defeat the German and Austro-Hungarian forces.

Chapter VIII

THE SECOND WORLD WAR

HISTORICAL BACKGROUND—EUROPE

*A*s noted at the end of the preceding chapter, the Treaty of Versailles which concluded the First World War contained the seeds of the Second World War. Both President Wilson of the United States and Prime Minister Lloyd George of Britain sought to moderate the French demands for reparations from Germany, but the French were adamant. The reparations, German disarmament, plus the demilitarization of the Rhineland, the loss to Germany of Alsace-Lorraine to France, the Sudetenland to Czechoslovakia, and part of East Prussia to Poland, led to a national paranoia exploited by Adolph Hitler.

In 1923 Hitler, along with General Erich Ludendorff, attempted to establish a military dictatorship with the "Beer Hall Putsch" in Munich. While in jail after this futile attempt, Hitler wrote *Mein Kampf*, which ultimately sold millions of copies and persuaded corresponding numbers of Germans that the Nazi party was the key to Germany regaining its past glory. In 1933, the Nazi Party won the last free German election with 44 percent of the total vote. With their right-wing National party allies, the Nazis could form a majority in the Reichstag, so President Hindenburg appointed Hitler as chancellor. Hitler then transformed the German democracy into a Nazi dictatorship, took Germany out of the League of

Nations, suppressed trade unions, and started the persecution of the Jews that would culminate in the Holocaust.

In Russia, the triumph of the Communist party over its rivals resulted in the formation of the Union of Soviet Socialist Republics in 1922. Josef Stalin assumed power after Lenin's death in 1924 and soon became an absolute dictator. He started the collectivization of individually owned farms, resulting in the liquidation of more than five million peasants and kulaks.

A third dictatorship was established by Benito Mussolini in Italy after his Fascist party came to power in 1922. In 1935, Italy invaded Ethiopia without a declaration of war. The League of Nations proved ineffective in suppressing the conflict, and Italy added Ethiopia to its other African colonies of Libya, Somaliland, and Eritrea.

Countering the trend to dictatorial government, the Spanish people deposed King Alfonso XIII in 1931 and established a republic. The republic, however, lost support from important factions by its attempts to limit the power of the Roman Catholic Church and reduce the gap between the rich and the poor. In 1936, the Spanish Civil War began. General Francisco Franco led the revolt against the new republic, ferrying troops from North Africa across the Strait of Gibraltar in German transport aircraft. Franco was further aided in the conflict by men and weapons from both Nazi Germany and Fascist Italy. The popular front government of the republic was supported by Russia and an international force, which included the Lincoln Brigade of U.S. volunteers. This dress rehearsal for the Second World War ended with Franco's victory in early 1939.[1]

However, it was the actions of Germany under Adolf Hitler that eventually led to the Second World War. Using as an excuse the signing of a pact between France and the Soviet Union in February 1936, Hitler ordered the reoccupation of the demilitarized Rhineland (demilitarization was one of the provisions of the Treaty of Versailles) on March 7,

1936. According to the British historian S.J.P. Taylor, "Hitler assured his protesting generals that he would withdraw his token force at the first sign of French action." The French ministry met with General Maurice Gamelin, the French chief of staff, who advised the government that France could only win the resulting war with support from Britain. When asked by France, Britain refused to support any action against Germany on the basis that British public opinion would not allow it. The matter was referred to the League of Nations, which declined to impose sanctions on Germany but did ask Hitler to propose a new security arrangement for Europe. Hitler proposed a twenty-five-year nonaggression pact, but the proposal died in committee. In retrospect, challenging Hitler over the Rhineland occupation could have been the move that would have forestalled his further aggressive actions.[2]

Two years later, German troops crossed into Austria, and Hitler declared the union of the two nations. The next crisis came over the Sudeten Germans in Czechoslovakia. Both France and Britain decided that they were not willing to start a war to prevent Hitler from annexing the Sudetenland. In Munich, Czechoslovakia was compelled by Neville Chamberlain of Britain and Edouard Daladier of France to accept a proposal put forward by Italy's Mussolini that essentially granted all of Hitler's demands. Chamberlain announced on September 30, 1938, that he had achieved "peace with honor."[3]

However, the problem of the city of Danzig remained. By the Treaty of Versailles, Danzig had been established as a free city at the end of the Polish corridor, giving Poland access to the Baltic Sea. The population of Danzig was largely German, and the Senate of the Free City came under Nazi domination. Poland, of course, opposed any German control of Danzig. In preparation for the possible showdown between Poland and Germany, both Hitler and the western alliance of Britain and France sought agreements with the

Soviet Union. Hitler succeeded, and on August 23, 1939, Germany and the Soviet Union signed a mutual nonaggression treaty. When Hitler heard the news, he is reported to have shouted, "Now Europe is mine. The others can have Asia!" Hitler hoped that he could repeat his success at Munich by intimidating the Poles into conceding Danzig. On August 29, he told the British diplomat Neville Henderson that he would negotiate directly with Poland if Poland sent an emissary the following day. When the Poles refused to send the emissary, the Germans published their terms—the immediate return of Danzig and a plebiscite on the Polish Corridor. In spite of the urging of the British, the Poles still refused to negotiate, and at 4:45 AM on August 30 the German attack on Poland began.[4]

At first both France and Britain hoped that a Europe-wide war could still be averted. When on August 31 Mussolini proposed a European conference to be held on September 5, the reaction of both the British and French governments was favorable. However, British public opinion was strongly in favor of giving Hitler an ultimatum to withdraw. Neville Chamberlain had to agree, and when Hitler ignored a September 3 ultimatum, the British declared war the same day. The French also entered the war on September 3. With the help of a Soviet invasion from the east, the Germans completely defeated the Poles in less than a month. Meanwhile, French soldiers sat behind the Maginot Line, and the first British force did not arrive on the continent until after Poland was lost.[5]

HISTORICAL BACKGROUND—FAR EAST

Japan started the first of its series of aggressions in 1931 when its troops conquered the China's northeastern province of Manchuria and renamed it Manchukuo. China protested to the League of Nations. The League set up a commission of inquiry, which deplored the use of force by Japan but did not recommend any punitive actions. The

United States proposed a policy of nonrecognition of any gains achieved through military conquest but did not follow this with a trade boycott. China did institute an economic boycott against Japan, but in 1932 the Japanese landed troops in Shanghai and forced China to abandon this policy.

The Japanese envisioned a "Greater Asian Co-Prosperity Sphere" throughout the Far East. They invaded mainland China in 1937, quickly conquered Peking and laid siege to Nanking, the provisional capital of the Chinese leader Chiang Kai-shek. Their conquest of that city later in 1937 is known as the Rape of Nanking because of the brutality of the Japanese troops. The Japanese advances also led to temporary cooperation between Chiang Kai-shek's forces, known as the Kuomintang, and the Communists under Mao Tsetung, whom Chiang had been trying to exterminate.[6]

The outbreak of war in Europe in 1939 interrupted the arms flow to the Kuomintang from Germany. At the demand of the Japanese, the British also closed the Burma highway, which was the main supply route of Soviet arms to the Communists. When the United States entered the war in 1941 after the bombing of Pearl Harbor, Chiang Kai-shek no longer saw any need for alliance with the Communists. Clashes between the two forces continued until 1945.[7]

UNITED STATES ENTRY INTO THE SECOND WORLD WAR

During 1939 and 1940, the United States maintained a position of neutrality. The historian Hanson Baldwin says, "Public sentiment supported the allies by a considerable majority but was also overwhelmingly opposed to participating in actual shooting war."[8] President Franklin D. Roosevelt, however, took a number of steps to aid the Allies, particularly Britain. Starting in 1940, shipments of so-called surplus arms, including 500,000 Enfield rifles, started to flow across the Atlantic. Britain also asked for destroyers, and fifty were transferred under a ships-for-bases arrangement that gave the United States bases in a series of islands from the Bahamas to Trinidad, as well as in Bermuda, and Newfoundland. In 1941, the U.S. Navy started convoy operations, escorting merchant ships part way across the Atlantic, where British naval vessels picked up the convoy. On October 17, one of the convoying destroyers, the *USS Kearny*, was hit by a German torpedo and 11 American seamen were killed, the first American casualties of the Second World War. Later that same month, another destroyer, the *Reuben Jones*, was sunk with 113 crew members lost. Although the United States was still officially neutral, in practice, the Navy was at war with Germany.

All semblance of neutrality disappeared when the Japanese attacked Pearl Harbor on December 7, 1941. There were extensive investigations of how the Japanese were able to achieve such complete surprise, and it was found that some communications from the Japanese had been decoded in Washington but not shared with the commanders at Pearl Harbor. From this, some revisionist historians constructed a theory that President Roosevelt deliberately misled his military commanders in order to secure U.S. entry into World War II. However, as the years pass and the hatred for Roosevelt fades into history, this conspiracy theory seems increasingly absurd.

On December 8, 1941, the day after the Pearl Harbor attack, Roosevelt asked Congress for a formal recognition of the existence of a state of war against Japan. A resolution to that effect was immediately passed with only one negative vote. from pacifist representative Jeannette Rankin of Montana. Three days later, Adolf Hitler declared war on the United States, and Italy quickly followed. On that same day, December 11, 1941, Congress recognized that a state of war existed with Italy and Germany.[9]

OUTCOME OF THE SECOND WORLD WAR

Both Germany and Japan were decisively defeated by the Allies. In Reims, France, on May 7, 1945, the Germans agreed to complete surrender of all their forces; the Japanese surrender followed on August 15, 1945.

American dead in the Second World War totaled 405,399. The cost of the war to the United States, excluding debt interest and veterans' benefits was about $315 billion (in current dollars.)

Probably the most important outcome of the Second World War was the establishment of the United Nations. The United Nations Declaration was signed on January 1, 1942, soon after the attack on Pearl Harbor, by the United States, Britain, the Soviet Union, China, and 22 other nations, with 20 more signatories added later. The signatories pledged to employ their full resources to defeat Germany and Japan and not to make a separate armistice or peace. When the German surrender drew near, a conference of 50 nations, including all the signatories of the declaration, was held in San Francisco commencing April 1945 to draft the United Nations Charter. Despite some disagreements between the East and the West, the charter was unanimously approved on June 20, 1945. Over the years, the membership has increased to more than 140 countries. Although the original focus of the organization was on the maintenance of peace, the East-West differences prevented most activities in this area during the first 40 years of the United Nations' existence. Nevertheless, the ancillary bodies such as the World Health Organization and the World Bank have made significant contributions to human welfare. In recent years, the peacekeeping efforts of the United Nations in Cyprus, Angola, Cambodia, and El Salvador have shown the possibility of conflict resolution through international efforts.

WARS UNNECESSARY FOR THE AGGRESSOR

COMPARISONS BETWEEN U.S., GERMANY, AND JAPAN

Country/ Statistic	Germany	Japan	United States
Form of Government	Parliament/ Democracy	Parliament/ Democracy	Republic/ Democracy
GNP per Capita (1989)[1]	$19,000	$23,040	$21,082
Inflation Rate (1990)[3]	2.8%	3.1%	5.4%
Unemployment Rate (1990)[3]	7.1% West 3.0% East	2.1%	5.5%
Divorce Rate/1-000[2]	2.1	1.4	4.8
Homicides per 100,000[2]	4.5	1.5	7.9
Infant Mortality/-1000[1]	6.0	4.0	10.0
Life Expectancy[1] (M/F)	73/81	75/81	73/80
Health Care	National	National	Private.

SOURCES:
1. *Countries of the World Yearbook, 1992* (Detroit: Gale Research)
2. Kurian, George, *The New Book of World Rankings* (New York: Facts on File, 1991)
3. C.I.A., *The World Fact Yearbook* (U.S. Govt. Printing Office, 1991)

United States Secretary of State General George C. Marshall, in 1947, offered economic aid to all the European nations, including the Soviet Union and it satellites. The Soviet Union refused the help and insisted its allies follow its example, but the Marshall Plan aid was a major factor in the recovery of Germany from the damages of the war. U.S. aid was also a significant factor in the recovery of Japan. In September 1951, a peace treaty was signed between Japan and most of the nations that had been at war with it (excluding the Soviet Union), which declared that "the Japanese people forever renounce war as a sovereign right of the nation, and the threat and use of force as a means of settling international disputes."[10]

WAS THIS WAR NECESSARY FOR THE AGGRESSORS?

As in the case of the First World War, the Second World War achieved none of the aims of the aggressors. Germany did not succeed in dominating Europe, nor did Japan in dominating Asia.

However, as many observers have noted, both Germany and Japan seem to have won in peace what they failed to win in war. The table on the opposite page, which is similar to the table in Chapter V, compares Germany, Japan, and the United States in a number of categories. Economically, the two other nations appear to have caught up with or surpassed the United States, whereas their social conditions, to the degree that they can be measured by statistics, appear superior to ours.

Some may claim that the German and Japanese economic performance is the result of United States aid. However, this aid was minor in comparison to the destruction of their industrial complex and infrastructure by the war, to say nothing of the loss of a generation of skilled manpower. It seems to me very likely that if both countries in 1940 had set goals for economic dominance, rather than for territorial expansion, they would be far ahead of their present performance.

Accordingly, I classify this war as unnecessary for the aggressors.

However, as in the case of the First World War, the Second World War, once it was initiated by the Axis powers, became a necessary war for Britain, France and, eventually, the United States. Even without the Japanese attack on Pearl Harbor, it would have been impossible for us to remain isolationist when the fate of Western Europe depended on our entry into the war. From the perspective of fifty years, for the United States it was a noble and just war, as well as a necessary one.

Chapter IX

THE KOREAN WAR

HISTORICAL BACKGROUND

*K*orea, although under the influence of China, had its own dynastic rulers from 1392 to 1910. Chinese influence was weakened by the Sino-Japanese War of 1894-1895, which was fought primarily over which power would dominate the peninsula and was won decisively by the Japanese. This war was followed by the Russo-Japanese War, again won by the Japanese. The Treaty of Portsmouth at the conclusion of this war acknowledged Japan's right to intervene in Korean internal affairs. Japan formally annexed Korea in 1910, giving it the ancient name of Chosen, and ruled it for the next 35 years.[1]

Korea was a minor issue in the discussions between the Allies during the Second World War. In December 1943, President Franklin Roosevelt, Prime Minister Winston Churchill, and Generalissimo Chiang Kai-shek issued the Cairo Declaration, which included a promise of Korean independence "in due course," with the declaration later approved by Soviet Premier Josef Stalin in Teheran. As the end of the Second World War approached, the Potsdam Conference in July 1945 resulted in a joint statement by President Harry Truman and Premier Stalin assuring Korea its independence after a five-year trusteeship.[2]

WARS UNNECESSARY FOR THE AGGRESSOR

In 1945, the coordinating function now performed by the National Security Council was vested in the State-War-Navy Coordinating Committee. The decision to propose to the Soviet Union that Korea should be split at the 38th parallel for occupation purposes was not taken until August 10, 1945, when this committee realized that the Soviet army was approaching Korea. Although some members of the committee pointed out that if the Soviets rejected the proposal, their army could occupy the whole peninsula before we could land our first soldiers, the Soviets accepted and stopped their advance at the agreed line on August 26. In fact, it was two weeks later before the first American troops reached Seoul.[3]

UNITED STATES INVOLVEMENT IN KOREA

One of the first task of the Americans after their occupation was to establish a new government for South Korea. For this, they turned to Dr. Syngman Rhee, a seventy-year-old Korean nationalist who had spent most of his life in the United States. After receiving an M.A. degree from Harvard and a Ph.D. from Princeton, he spent the period between 1910 and 1945 lobbying for the cause of Korean independence. The U.S. State Department initially refused to grant him a passport, since it regarded him as a dangerous troublemaker. However, in spite of the department's reservations, Rhee was brought back to Korea by the U.S. Military Government in one of General Douglas MacArthur's aircraft. He arrived in time to participate in the official welcome for the American troops, held in Seoul on October 20, 1945.[4] In December 1945 a conference held in Moscow set up a five-year period of trusteeship for Korea, with the United States, the Soviet Union, Britain, and China, as trustees. The conference also agreed to the establishment of a provisional democratic government. However, when the trustees could not agree on details of the election of this unified government, both sides set up their own governments in their own zones. In the north, a single-party election led to the communist People's Democratic Republic. In the south, a legislative assembly was set up in December 1946 with half of the members elected and the other half appointed.

The following year, the United States brought the Korean situation to the General Assembly of the United Nations, where the Soviets did not have a veto, and a majority of the members were favorable to the U.S. point of view. In spite of Soviet objections, the General Assembly voted on November 14, 1947, to set up a new UN commission to supervise country-wide elections leading to an independent, unified country. However, North Korea refused admission to the UN commission. The commission then recommended, and the General Assembly approved, elections in South Korea. The leftist elements in the country opposed the election. Syngman Rhee's forces retaliated, and 323 people were killed in riots and police raids in the ten days prior to elections. An overwhelming majority of the seats in the National Legislative Assembly were won by the rightist parties. Syngman Rhee became the first president of the Republic of Korea, and the new republic was established on August 15, 1948.[5]

Both the United States and the Soviet Union now withdrew their forces from the Korean peninsula. The United States left behind only a 500-man assistance and training group, the KMAG. The United Nations Commission on Korea, still charged with the responsibility of unifying the divided country, maintained a presence in South Korea and monitored the hostile activities of both sides. The Soviet Union supplied North Korea with large amounts of artillery, tanks, and military aircraft. The United States deliberately denied similar weapons to South Korea for fear that Syngman Rhee might initiate a war with the north.

Syngman Rhee faced considerable opposition in the south and was not hesitant in trying to quash it. He dismissed any minister who showed signs of independence, restricted freedom of the press, carried out a series of political arrests, and arranged for the assassination of his principle rival, Kim Ku. In the elections held in May 1950, less than two months before the North Korean invasion, Syngman's Rhee's party and his allies won only 49 out of the 223 seats.[6] A week before the attack, the intelligence unit at the U.S. General Headquarters in Tokyo reported to Washington, "Apparently Soviet advisers believe that now is the opportune time to attempt to subjugate the south by political means."[7] In view of the unpopularity of Syngman Rhee, it seems possible that North Korea could have achieved its aims through subversion and guerrilla warfare rather than an outright attack. In his book on the Korean War, the British author Max Hastings quotes a South Korean officer as having said after the war, "If Kim [Kim Il Sung, the North Korean leader] really wanted to get the South, by far his best course would have been to do nothing. His biggest mistake was to attack us." Hastings goes on to say, "A few more years of discreet subversion should have ensured collapse from within."

However, Kim had determined on attack. He went to Moscow and received Stalin's acquiescence, if not outright support, for his plans. The Chinese were also probably passive rather than active partners in North Korea's intentions.[8]

The North Korean attack began at 4:00 AM on Sunday, June 25, 1950, with an artillery and mortar attack. On June 28 they captured the South Korean capitol, Seoul. In the meantime, the United States, requested that UN Secretary-General Trygve Lie call an emergency meeting of the Security Council. At this time, the Soviet Union was boycotting the Security Council its of their refusal to replace the Nationalist China delegation with Communist China representatives. In the Soviet absence, the United Nations passed a resolution on June 25 condemning the North Korean attack and demanding its withdrawal to the 38th parallel. A second resolution calling on member nations to "render such assistance to the Republic of Korea as may be necessary to repel the armed attack and restore peace and security to the area" was passed by the Security Council on June 27. The United Nations also agreed to a unified command under a U.S. commander, who would report back periodically to the Security Council. President Harry Truman chose not to go to Congress to ask for a declaration of war on the basis that we were repelling a "bandit incursion" and that the powers of the Presidency, combined with the mandate from the United Nations, were sufficient bases for his actions.[9]

By July 1, the first units of the 21st Infantry Regiment reached Korea from its base in Japan. The unit engaged the enemy on July 5, 1950, thus striking the first blow for the United Nations in what was even then called a new world order. The United States. was soon fully involved in this undeclared war.

OUTCOME OF THE WAR

In the election campaign of 1952 between Dwight Eisenhower and Adlai Stevenson, Eisenhower pledged to "concentrate on the job of ending the Korean War," including going to Korea. In part because of this pledge, Eisenhower carried all but nine states. In December, the President-elect fulfilled his pledge by going to Korea and talking with some of the line commanders and their troops. Apparently, he decided that there was no sense in endless battles over barren real estate. However, armistice negotiations, which had started on July 10, 1951, were going nowhere. Although it may have been a coincidence, after Stalin's death on March 5, 1953, progress was made. An agreement to exchange sick and wounded prisoners was signed on April 11, with an agreement on the rest of the prisoners concluded on June 8. Fighting continued while negotiation dragged on. In negotiating, the United States not only had to reach an agreement with the North Koreans but also with the South Koreans, since Syngman Rhee was bitterly opposed to ending the war without having unified the country under his control. However, under threat of abandonment by the United States, Rhee finally caved in, and an armistice was signed on July 27, 1953. With some slight rectification of the border between the north and the south, the *status quo ante bellum* was restored.

In the war, 33,629 American soldiers died, with a further 105,785 wounded. The South Koreans lost 415,000 killed and 429,000 wounded. North Korean and Chinese casualties probably exceeded 1.5 million. The total cost of the war to the United States was about $79 billion, excluding debt interest and veterans' benefits.[10]

One result of the war was to enhance the prestige of the United Nations. General Matthew Ridgeway, who followed Douglas MacArthur as Supreme Commander for the Far East, stated: "I believe military history offers no parallel of so many allies serving side by side in battle so harmoniously.... I have no hesitancy in saying that the presence of these troops [UN] has greatly enhanced the effectiveness of the United Nations Command."

Finally, the war provided a basis for the economic development of Korea that has led to its position as one of the greatest economic and political powers in Asia. In terms of the classification used by economists, it is no longer a "less developed country (LDC)" but a "newly industrialized country (NIC)." The contrast with North Korea is similar to the contrast between West Germany and the former German Democratic Republic in East Germany.

WAS THIS WAR NECESSARY FOR THE AGGRESSORS?

North Korea's obvious intention when it launched its attack on June 25, 1950, was to conquer South Korea. Since it failed in that objective, the war was unnecessary under the first of the criteria established in the introductory chapter.

However, as pointed out earlier in this chapter, the war may also have been unnecessary because of the possibility of North Korea achieving its goals by patiently waiting for the South Korean government to collapse from the revulsion of the people over Syngman Rhee's dictatorial methods. Even if there had not been a complete collapse, a coalition of leftist parties might have replaced Rhee's rightist regime and been willing to negotiate with the Communists. However, Kim Il Sung's attack unified the south and brought in the United States, which still has a military presence in South Korea forty years later.

For both these reasons, I believe that this was an unnecessary war for the aggressor, North Korea.

WAS THIS WAR NECESSARY FOR THE UNITED STATES?

The reader will have noticed that the Vietnam War was included in the section of Probably Unnecessary Wars, whereas the Korean War is in the section of Wars Unnecessary for the Aggressor. This implies that although it was probably not necessary for the United States to be involved in Vietnam, it _was_ necessary for the United States to help the South Koreans.

The difference between the two situations seems to me to be in the degree of commitment of the United States to the two regimes. In the case of Korea, the United States had established the line of demarcation between the north and the south, had instituted the government, and had maintained a military presence through the KMAG. Thus, when North Korea attacked, we had a moral obligation to aid the country we had established. In Vietnam, on the other hand, we had no moral obligation to replace the French. In Korea, the war was precipitated by a clear-cut act of aggression. In Vietnam, we stepped into the middle of a continuing civil war.

Finally, in Korea we acted through the United Nations, which ensured an international consensus (excluding the Soviet Union and its allies) on the justification for our actions to counter the aggression. There was no such consensus on Vietnam; Britain would not even furnish a token contingent when President Lyndon Johnson requested its support.

Although there was disappointment in some U.S. quarters that we did not "win" the Korean War, the United States did achieve its limited objective of preventing the conquest of the south. It was the first U.S. experience in fighting a limited war. By limiting our aims and compromising on the final armistice, it remained a just war fought to repel an aggressor. However, if we had fought an all-out war, including the use of nuclear weapons, as some urged, we could have initiated World War III—which would have been the ultimate unnecessary war!

OBVIOUSLY

UNNECESSARY

WARS

Chapter IX

THREE POTENTIAL WARS THAT WERE AVOIDED

A s mentioned in the Introduction, a war can be said to be obviously unnecessary if the desired results could be achieved without hostilities. This chapter examines two minor and one major crises that fall in this category, since potentially they could have led to war, but were resolved peacefully.

"FIFTY-FOUR FORTY OR FIGHT"

Originally, the Oregon Territory referred to all the land between the Rocky Mountains and the Pacific, from California on the south to the Russian border (now Alaska) on the north, which was at latitude 54° 40´. In the early part of the nineteenth century, the territory was claimed by both Great Britain and the United States by virtue of discovery, exploration, and settlement. By a treaty between the United States and Great Britain referred to as the Convention of 1818, the two parties agreed in that year to joint occupation for ten years; the agreement was extended indefinitely in 1826.

There the matter stood until 1843, when a convention on the Oregon question held in Cincinnati adopted a resolution demanding that the territory up to the Russian boundary of 54° 40´ be ceded by Britain to the United States. The following year, Senator William Allen of Ohio coined the phrase "Fifty-four Forty or Fight!" in a speech on the Senate floor.

At the Democratic Presidential nominating convention in 1844, the favorite candidate was Martin Van Buren, who had been President from 1836 to 1840. However, Van Buren issued a statement opposing the annexation of Texas, and the nomination on the eighth ballot went to James Polk, an avowed expansionist who had been expected to be the Vice-Presidential candidate. The Democrats incorporated into their platform a demand for the "re-annexation of Texas and the re-occupation of Oregon," with the prefix "re" implying that all of Oregon was already rightfully ours. The Whig candidate, Henry Clay, at first opposed the annexation of Texas, though he issued a guarded pro-annexation statement after his nomination. Polk's unabashed expansionism on the questions both of Texas and Oregon won him the election.

In his inaugural address of March 4, 1845, President Polk stated, "Our title to the country of Oregon is clear and unmistakable."[1] He repeated this assertion in his first annual State of the Union message. Settlers heading west on the Oregon Trail painted "Fifty-four Forty" on their wagon covers. However, as it appeared possible that the annexation of Texas might lead to war with Mexico, the Administration decided that it did not want wars on two frontiers. The historian David Saville Muzzey states, "After a rather amusing campaign of correspondence in which the President and the Senate each tried to throw on the other the responsibility for deserting the platform, 'Fifty-four Forty or Fight,' a treaty was made with Great Britain (June, 1846.)"[2] The treaty provided for the continuation of the border east of the Rockies, which was the 49th parallel, west to the Pacific, with a jog at the end to give Vancouver Island to Canada. Britain also was granted the right of free navigation of the Columbia River from the Canadian border to the Pacific Ocean (which in the long run was not a very valuable right because of the hydroelectric dams that were established on the Columbia).

That the dispute was settled peacefully seems conclusive proof that the war demanded by the belligerent wing of the Democratic party was unnecessary.[3]

THE VENEZUELAN BOUNDARY CONTROVERSY

At the time that Great Britain annexed the territory of British Guiana in Central America in 1814, there was no firm boundary on the west with Venezuela. A line was finally established in 1840 by a British agent named Robert Schomburgh. This was claimed as the boundary by the British, though Venezuela disputed it. Then in 1885, when gold and other minerals were reported west of this line, Britain claimed an additional 23,000 square miles beyond the Schomburgh boundary. Venezuela protested and broke off relations in February 1887.

The United States felt that the British action came under the Monroe Doctrine of 1823, which declared that the continent was closed to any further extensions of the European colonial system. The U.S. State Department urged Britain to arbitrate its claims, but Britain refused to accept the applicability of the Monroe Doctrine or even that the United States had a legitimate interest in the settlement of its dispute with Venezuela. There were several more exchanges of notes, and in December 1895, President Grover Cleveland placed the matter before Congress. In his message, he reviewed the exchanges of notes with the British, asked for an appropriation for an investigative commission, and stated:

> When such report is made and accepted it will, in my opinion, be the duty of the United States to resist by every means in its power, as a willful aggression upon its rights and interests, the appropriation of any lands or the exercise of governmental jurisdiction over any

territory which after investigation we have determined of right belongs to Venezuela. In making these recommendations, I am fully alive to the responsibility incurred and keenly realize all the consequences which may follow.[4]

The possible consequences, of course, included war with Great Britain. Congress accepted the recommendations by a unanimous vote and appropriated $100,000 for an investigatory commission. Historian Henry Steele Commanger comments, "To many it seemed that war was inevitable."[5] Theodore Roosevelt, then a police commissioner for New York City, wrote to his friend Senator Henry Cabot Lodge, "Personally, I rather hope that the fight will come soon. The clamor of the peace faction has convinced me that this country needs war. Let the fight come if it must; I don't care whether our sea coast cities are bombarded or not; we would take Canada."[6] (As recounted in Chapter III, two years later Senator Lodge and Roosevelt, then Assistant Secretary of the Navy, worked to involve the United States in the Spanish-American War.)

However, when the British people found out about President Cleveland's message and the action of Congress, they immediately protested the possibility of war with the United States. Three hundred and fifty members of Parliament sent a petition to Cleveland asking that all disputes between the two nations be settled by arbitration. The British prime minister, Lord Salisbury, backed down, and in February 1897 the United States and Great Britain signed a treaty that provided for the British claim in Venezuela to be submitted to arbitration at an international tribunal in Paris. The decision handed down by the tribunal in October 1899 fixed the disputed boundary along a line that was generally favorable to the British claim.[7]

That the British government is willing to fight for what it believes are its territorial rights in this hemisphere was shown by the Falklands War in this century. In the Venezuela incident in 1895-1896, the United States was ready to send in the marines to enforce the Monroe Doctrine. As noted above, there was popular support for doing so. However, there was no such popular support in Britain for a war. The subsequent peaceful settlement shows that this was an obviously unnecessary war.

THE CUBAN MISSILE CRISIS
HISTORICAL BACKGROUND

On March 10, 1952, General Fulgencio Batista of Cuba led a coup that ousted the elected president and established a pro-American government that was immediately recognized by the United States. The coup was also immediately denounced by a young law school graduate named Fidel Castro. He filed a brief with the Cuban Court of Constitutional Guarantees (which played a role similar to that of the U.S. Supreme Court) asking that Batista's seizure of power be declared unconstitutional. When no attention was paid to the suit, he decided to overthrow the Batista regime by revolution.

Castro organized a group of like-minded revolutionaries. Their first attempt to overthrow the government was an attack on the Moncada barracks in the center of the city of Santiago de Cuba on July 26, 1953. This ended in failure. Castro was captured, tried, and sentenced to fifteen years in the Isle of Pines prison. He was released in May 1955 as part of a general amnesty for political prisoners. He went to Mexico and prepared to invade Cuba, which he did on December 2, 1956. The invasion boat landed in a mangrove swamp on the southeastern coast, and the men had to abandon their arms to reach dry land. They headed for the Sierra Maestra mountains. There Castro, his brother Raoul, and Ernesto "Che" Guevara, an Argentine revolutionary, led a growing band of guerrilla fighters, who were supported in part by anti-Batista Cuban exiles in Miami. By the end of 1958, Castro and his followers were in a position to attack the Batista forces directly. After the revolutionary forces won a series of striking victories against numerically superior government forces, Batista left Cuba on January 1, 1959. Castro immediately seized the reins of power.

Initially, the attitude of the United States toward the new regime was conciliatory. The American ambassador, Philip Bonsal, worked to keep Cuba within the American sphere of influence, not realizing the depth of Castro's anti-American feelings, stemming from the previous U.S. support of the Batista regime. From all reports, Castro was not a Communist in 1959, but he certainly believed in social reform. His actions, such as expropriation and redistribution of land, was interpreted by the United States as pure Communism. When the British, responding to U.S. pressure, refused to sell arms to Cuba, Castro then turned to the Soviets, who were happy to do so. Nevertheless, diplomatic relations between the United States and Cuba continued, and in April 1960, Castro appointed a new ambassador to the United States.

By that time, though, the United States was helping train a group of Cuban exiles for an invasion of Cuba. In the election campaign of 1960, both Richard Nixon and John F. Kennedy endorsed an invasion by anti-Castro exiles. After his election, Kennedy learned in briefings of the planned invasion and approved continuation of the training. Castro too learned of the invasion plan and demanded that Washington reduce the staff at its Havana embassy. President Eisenhower, in one of his last acts, broke off relations with Cuba. After the January 20, 1961, inauguration of President Kennedy, invasion plans continued. On April 17, an invasion force of about 15,000 men, assisted by the U.S. Navy and the C.I.A., landed at the Bay of Pigs. The invasion force was decisively defeated, and 1,180 of the 1,297 men who landed were taken prisoner. The prisoners were well treated and were later ransomed by the United States in return for medical supplies to Cuba.[8]

A year later, Castro feared that there would be another invasion. Thus, when the Soviet Premier Nikita Khrushchev proposed sending missiles to Cuba to act as deterrence to American hostile actions, Castro readily accepted. Khrushchev apparently believed that the installation of the missiles could be concealed from the United States until they were fully deployed. By October 1962, the Soviets had delivered 42 medium-range ballistic nuclear missiles to Cuba, as well as 6 tactical missile launchers, with 9 nuclear warheads. Although the control over the launching of strategic weapons remained in Moscow, the local Soviet field commanders had authority to launch the tactical weapons in case of a U.S. invasion.[9]

Initially, the Soviet Union and Cuba were successful in keeping the delivery and the installation of the weapons a secret. On several occasions during September 1962, the Soviets assured the United States that they had no intention of sending surface-to-surface missiles to Cuba. Thus, when pictures taken by an American U-2 spy plane on October 14, 1962, clearly showed missiles being installed, the Kennedy Administration was taken by complete surprise.[10]

At 11:45 AM on October 16, the Central Intelligence Agency briefed the Executive Committee of the National Security Council, known as ExComm. This consisted of a group of high officials, including the President, Attorney General Robert F. Kennedy, Secretary of Defense Robert F. McNamara, and Secretary of State Dean Rusk. At the first meeting of the committee, the President outlined four courses of action, all involving some kind of air strike against Cuba. Robert Kennedy suggested a fifth option — invasion. By the time of a meeting held later that day, the president had reduced the options to three: a surgical air strike, a more general bombardment, and an invasion. At that point, General Maxwell Taylor, Chairman of the Joint Chiefs of Staff, broached the idea of a blockade around Cuba as part of the strategy for invasion, and Robert McNamara suggested that the blockade was an option in its own right. At this meeting, Robert Kennedy proposed that some pretext might be found for an invasion, in the same way that the sinking of the battleship *Maine* had served as a pretext for the Spanish-American War.[11]

Meetings continued throughout the week. Initially, the majority of the participants favored a surgical air strike. However, the Air Force pointed out that the strike could not be limited to the missile sites but must include the destruction of Soviet fighter planes and bombers. Further, massive bombardment of not only the ballistic missile sites but also of short-range missile sites and artillery, which could attack our naval base at Guantanamo Bay, would be required. The participants concluded that the resulting chaos would necessitate an invasion. The blockade option gained favor, since it offered Khrushchev the choice of avoiding direct military action by keeping his ships away. However, it was decided initially to let tankers carrying petroleum, oil, and lubricants through the blockade.[12]

At 5:00 PM on Monday, October 22, 1962, President Kennedy met with congressional leaders, whom he had summoned back to Washington from their election campaigns, and informed them of the Soviet missile buildup and his proposed blockade. Both Senator Richard Russell, the chairman of the Senate Armed Services Committee, and Senator William Fulbright, the chairman of the Senate Foreign Relations Committee, reacted forcibly against the Administration's planned blockade, proposing instead an immediate invasion of Cuba. The President explained why he had decided against this hawkish approach, and Senator Everett Dirksen, Senate minority leader, expressed his support of the President's plan.[13]

At 7:00 PM the President in a television address informed the American people of the secret buildup of Soviet offensive missiles in Cuba. His speech said in part:

The 1930's taught us a clear lesson: aggressive conduct, if allowed to go unchecked and unchallenged, ultimately leads to war. This nation is opposed to war. We are also true to our word. Our unswerving objective, therefore, must be to prevent the use of these missiles against this or any other country, and to secure their withdrawal or elimination from the Western Hemisphere....

He went on to outline the steps he proposed to take: quarantine, surveillance of the buildup. reinforcement of the Guantanamo Bay naval base, and appeals to the Castro and Khrushchev. He did not set a time limit for compliance nor threaten any specific retaliation for noncompliance. He concluded with a plea for peace and freedom. The speech was broadcast around the world in thirty-eight languages.[14]

The reaction abroad was mixed. The British press was largely negative, and the eminent philosopher Bertrand Russell cabled the President, "Your action desperate.....no conceivable justification." However, on October 23, the Organization of American States unanimously adopted a resolution supporting the quarantine. Washington also received strong support at the United Nations for its actions after a capable presentation of the evidence of Soviet perfidy by Ambassador Adlai Stevenson.

At the time of the quarantine, eighteen Soviet dry cargo ships were headed toward Cuba. Intelligence reports indicated that they were accompanied by six Soviet submarines. United Nations Secretary General U Thant urged both sides to avoid contact. On Wednesday, October 24, two days after the President's speech, the Soviet ships headed for Cuba stopped, and then during the next two days turned around and headed back to the Soviet Union. To the United States, it seemed likely that the Soviets did not want to risk having their secret military hardware aboard these ships seized by the U.S. Navy. However, the crisis was not over, for the Soviets continued work on the installation of the ballistic missiles already in Cuba. On the U.S. side, planes ready for an air strike and a force ready for invasion were assembled in Florida.

On Friday, October 26, the President received a private letter from Khrushchev that seemed to contain the basis for a settlement. The premier He stated that since the Soviet missiles were placed in Cuba as a defense against possible U.S. invasion, they would be withdrawn under UN inspection if the United States agreed not to invade Cuba. However, a public message from the Soviets the following day made no mention of this proposal and demanded that the United States remove its missiles from Turkey.

On the same day, October 27, a U.S. spy plane was shot down over Cuba by a Soviet surface-to-air missile. In accordance with standing orders to immediately destroy a Cuban site firing a missile, General Curtis LeMay ordered that F-100 fighter-bombers be readied for a strike. Before the planes took off, however, the White House countermanded the order. LeMay's reaction was, "He chickened out again." In any case, LeMay put the Strategic Air Command on war footing, with a substantial portion of the strategic bombers in the air. In all, 1,576 bombers and 286 missiles were poised to strike the Soviet Union.[15]

While these military preparations were underway, discussions continued at the White House on how to reply to Khrushchev's contradictory messages. It was decided by the President to ignore the second letter and accept the proposal in the private message. A reply was drafted by Robert Kennedy and Ted Sorensen, the Special Counsel to the President and one of his most influential advisers. The message was reviewed with Ambassador Stevenson, and transmitted to Moscow at 8:00 PM that night. The same evening, Robert Kennedy met with the Soviet ambassador in Washington and relayed the contents of the President's letter, asking for a reply the next day. The following morning the Soviets announced in a public broadcast that Khrushchev had accepted Kennedy's proposal. This should have ended the crisis, but Robert Kennedy in his book *Thirteen Days* reports, "One of the Joint Chiefs of Staff once said to me he believed in a preventive attack against the Soviet Union. On that fateful Sunday morning when the Russians announced they were withdrawing their missiles, it was suggested by one high military adviser that we attack Monday in any case."[16]

Subsequently, the Soviets carried out their agreement to remove the missiles, and the United States has honored its pledge not to invade Cuba. The United States also quietly removed the obsolete Jupiter missiles from Turkey.

In all three of the crises reviewed in this chapter, the role of the President was crucial. In each case, the President stood up to pressures for military action from politicians in his own party. Presidents Polk, Cleveland, and Kennedy all had the inner strength to reject the arguments of the hawks and to see that the true national interest lay in a peaceful solution to the conflict. The next chapter will attempt to draw some conclusions from the eight major wars that the United States has fought, as well as from these three potential wars, which were averted.

CONCLUSIONS

Chapter XI

PATIENCE AND FORTITUDE

*O*n the basis of the eight wars and three almost wars described in this book, one ought to be able to draw some conclusions on how to avoid unnecessary wars. Of course, any conclusions must be viewed in the light of the changes that have taken place in diplomatic relations and warfare over the two-hundred-year span covered in the preceding chapters.

Nevertheless, one can make some general observations. It seems likely that most of the wars described in this book could have been averted if the national leadership had shown more patience in continuing diplomatic negotiations and had been willing to stand up to the outcry for military action by the press and the hawkish politicians.

The degree of patience required varied from war to war. In the cases of the War of 1812 and the Spanish-American War, a delay of several weeks would almost certainly have allowed time for the news to arrive that the diplomatic negotiations had been successful and that the adversary had already capitulated on the principal point of difference (the War of 1812) or was willing to compromise on all significant outstanding issues (the Spanish-American War). The First World War might have been avoided if the Austrians had been willing to negotiate with the Serbs for another month. During the cold war following the Second World War, the United States and its allies patiently main-

CONCLUSIONS

tained an armed truce with the Soviet Union for more than forty years, in spite of calls from some hawkish politicians and military people for a preventive nuclear strike against the Soviets. The United States was eventually rewarded with a victory that we would not have achieved through war. Probably a similar or longer time period would have been required to achieve the aims of the American Revolution through negotiation rather than rebellion. However, based on the experiences in Canada, New Zealand, and Australia, the United States probably could have achieved effective independence without armed conflict over a time period not greatly exceeding that of the cold war.

Patience and diplomatic negotiations also effectively prevented two of the almost wars. The potential conflict resulting from the "Fifty-four Forty or Fight" agitation was defused by negotiations, both between the United States and Great Britain and between President James Polk and the U.S. Senate. The Cuban Missile Crisis was ended by skillful diplomacy on the part of President John F. Kennedy and members of his Administration, who resisted calls for the bombing or invasion of Cuba.

In addition to patiently continuing diplomatic negotiations, a key factor in avoiding unnecessary wars is determining the true national interest. Two of the other wars might have been avoided if the national leadership had taken a different view of the national interest. In the case of the Vietnam War, both John F. Kennedy and Lyndon Johnson initially regarded Vietnam as peripheral to U.S. interests. When he was a senator, Kennedy stated in November 1951, "In Indochina, we have allied ourselves to the desperate efforts of the French regime to hang on to the remnants of Empire." Lyndon Johnson, as majority leader of the Senate, refused to support President Dwight Eisenhower's proposed intervention in Vietnam in 1954. Kennedy and Johnson changed their minds only when they were convinced by their advisers that the North Vietnamese were part of a worldwide

Communist conspiracy to dominate the capitalist countries. In retrospect, the original views of Kennedy and Johnson—- that this was a struggle in a remote part of the world that did not involve the national interest—were correct. The second case of possible mistake in identifying the national interest is the Civil War. If Abraham Lincoln had foreseen that the Civil War would result in the loss of more than half a million lives, he might have decided that it was in the true national interest to let the South secede.

However, as the title of this chapter implies, avoiding war sometimes takes not only patience but also fortitude. The Second World War might have been avoided if the Allies had challenged Hitler when he first abrogated the Treaty of Versailles by reoccupying the Rhineland. Historians agree that he was prepared to back down if he had been challenged. American military strength and the threat of nuclear retaliation was an important factor in keeping the peace during the cold war.

The most recent United States war analyzed in this book was the Vietnam War. Since then, the United States had been involved militarily in Grenada, Panama, Iraq, and Somalia, though only the Iraq action was of sufficient magnitude to warrant being termed a war. All four conflicts are too recent to form the historical perspective required to decide whether they were necessary or not. However, there is a suspicion that at least some of these conflicts were caused by, rather than prevented by, the United States having a large standing military force. There surely must be a temptation for both the President and the Department of Defense to justify large military expenditures by demonstrating the usefulness of armed force, even in those instances in which the aims could have been accomplished by diplomacy or nonviolent measures such as blockades. Thus, fortitude is not necessarily a factor in preventing war. Moreover, it is clear that the United States is now the only military superpower in the world. If the President decides that the

CONCLUSIONS

national interest requires the use of U.S. military force anywhere in the world, there is no other power capable of really challenging him. As Theodore Draper pointed out in a recent article in *The New York Review of Books*, recent Presidents have ignored the constitutional provision that only Congress can declare war, so Presidential power to take military action has not in practice been tempered by congressional reluctance. The decision as to whether a war is necessary or not is, by default, the President's alone. Although the United Nations has been consulted and, in effect, used as a surrogate by the United States, this country has not relinquished the direction of any part of its armed forces to a United Nations command.

To many observers, this is not a satisfactory state of affairs. Remaining the only superpower imposes a heavy economic burden on the United States; the new Clinton administration proposes only minimal cuts in the 1997 "Base Force" budget of $250 billion proposed by the Department of Defense (even though this is a substantial reduction from the actual 1990 expenditures of $336 billion). Probably more important, reliance on one nation's military might does not build a system of collective security that might eventually eliminate war.

A number of proposals have been made for mechanisms to promote a more secure world order. One of the most comprehensive has been put forward by Randall Forsberg, the director of the Institute for Defense and Disarmament Studies in Cambridge, Massachusetts.

Forsberg has outlined a four-phase plan to build confidence in a cooperative security system:
1. In the first phase, the major industrial powers and the larger developing nations would announce that acts of aggression and genocide by any state would warrant a multilateral military response. While retaining the right to unilateral action, those powers would agree to try to organize multilateral action through the United Nations. They

would also agree that such action would require at least thirteen votes of the fifteen-member Security Council, that no more than half the troops would come from the major powers, and that the military command would be shared. Discussions would also take place between the major powers on how to stop civil wars and ethnic conflicts that do not qualify as aggressive wars or genocide.

2. The second phase would involve reductions in weapons inventories, combined with limitations on arms exports. The aim would be to reduce arms inventories to a new, lower level and then limit new procurement by both arms producers and non-producers to replacement of obsolete weapons on a one-for-one basis.

3. In the third phase, arms reductions would continue to the point that no major power, including the United States and Russia, would have unilateral military superiority in all possible conflicts. This would require multilateral cooperation to stop conflicts among the most heavily armed developing nations, such as the two Koreas or India and Pakistan. Phase three would be continued until all parties were satisfied that the multilateral mechanisms worked in practice.

4. In the fourth and final stage, all nations would reduce their forces to those required for defense of their national territory, plus rapid deployment forces on call from the United Nations. No single country would have the forces capable of launching a large-scale attack on another. Their combined forces could stop any civil war or ethnic conflict. The production and export of all major offensive weapons systems would be banned. Forsberg envisions that eventually the nations would agree that "violence should never be used except to the minimum extent needed to stop violence, and war should never be used to advance political or economic interests."[2]

In an earlier article, Forsberg estimated that this kind of approach to cooperative security eventually could lead to a United States defense budget as low as $70 billion per

CONCLUSIONS

year in the early years of the twenty-first century (compared with the 1990 actual expenditure of $336 billion and the defense department estimate of a 1997 budget of $251 billion.). Of this $70 billion, $5 billion would support ten strategic submarines, $1 billion would maintain the existing air defense system, $1 billion would cover the National Guard, and the remainder would support the U.S. complement of forces required for multilateral peacekeeping, including those on loan to a UN command and those maintained under U.S. command. This reduction in military expenditures would be accompanied by a correspondingly reduced risk to the lives of American soldiers, airmen, and sailors.[3]

Implicit in Forsberg's proposals is the continued role of the United Nations in deciding which conflicts require multilateral response and in the coordination of the military units involved in this response. Article 43 of the United Nations Charter states:

> All members...undertake to make available to the Security Council on its call and in accordance with a special agreement or agreements, armed forces, assistance and facilities, including right of passage, necessary for the purpose of maintaining international peace and security.

The special agreement required to implement this article has never been negotiated and signed. Along with the changes in the operation of the Security Council suggested by Forsberg, these agreements should now be drafted. In the case of the United States, this probably would require Congress to exercise its constitutional power to declare war by giving a blanket delegation of this power, under strict limitations, to the Security Council. The question of command of the UN forces also would have to be worked out. A recent report issued by the United Nations Association of the

U.S.A. suggests that the NATO command structure might serve as a model.[4]

A number of other ideas on how to eliminate conflicts are given in Robert Woito's 1982 book *To End War*. Although it is now somewhat dated, it serves as a good bibliography and reference on this subject up to 1982.[5]

In the past, patience and fortitude might have been sufficient to prevent the United States from embarking on unnecessary wars. In the future, it appears that we also shall need a willingness to work toward a system of cooperative security based on the United Nations that relieves us of our present position as the world's policeman. If such a system of cooperative security is established, it seems possible that eventually there will be no more wars—necessary or unnecessary!

SOURCES AND BIBLIOGRAPHIC NOTES

CHAPTER I INTRODUCTION
1. Walzer, Michael, *Just and Unjust Wars: A Moral Argument with Historical Illustrations* (New York: Basic Books, 1977).
2. Safire, William, *Safire's Political Dictionary* (New York: Random House, 1978}.
3. Thucydides, *History of the Peloponnesian War*, book VI, chapters 8-18. Translated by Benjamin Jowett. (New York: Random House, 1942).

CHAPTER II THE WAR OF 1812
1. Ryerson, Egerton, *The Loyalists of America and Their Times* (Toronto: W. Briggal, 1880), p.335.
2. Wise, Sidney F., "The War of 1812 in Popular History" in *War Along the Niagara* (Youngstown, NY: Old Fort Niagara Assoc. 1991), p.116.
3. Muzzey, David Saville, *An American History* (Boston: Ginn & Co, 1911), p.216.
4. Morison, Samuel Eliot, *The Oxford History of the American People* (New York: Oxford University Press, 1965), p.378.
5. James, William, *The Naval History of Great Britain*, Vol.IV (London: Macmillan and Co,, 1902), p.324.
6. Roosevelt, Theodore, *The Naval War of 1812*, vol.I (New York: G.P. Putnam's Sons, 1889), p.29.
7. Perkin, Bradford, *Prolgue to War* (Berkeley: University of California Press 1963), pp.88-95.
8. Morison, op.cit., p.381.
9. A well-written fictional account of the life of Tecumseh, including the battle of Tippecanoe is given in *Panther in the Sky* by James Alexander Thom (New York: Ballentine Books, 1989).

10. Cruikshank, Ernest, *The Battle of Ft. George* (Niagara-on-the-Lake: Niagara Historical Society, 1990), p.14-15.
11. Beard, Charles A. and Mary R., *The Rise of American Civilization*, vol.I (New York: Macmillan, 1939), p.410.
12. Ibid., p.412
13. Pratt, Julius W., *Expansionists of 1812* (New York: Macmillan, 1925), pp.50-59.
14. Beard, op.cit., p.410
15. Hickey, Donald R., *The War of 1812* (Urbana: University of Illinois Press, 1989), pp.29-30.
16. Remini, Robert V., *Henry Clay: Statesman for the Union* (New York: W.W. Norton, 1991), chapters 1 - 6.
17. Coit, Margaret L., *John C. Calhoun: American Portrait* (Boston: Houghton Mifflin, 1950), chapters I - VI.
18. Remini, Robert V., op.cit, pp.83-93.
19. Stagg, John Charles Anderson, *Mr. Madison's War* (Princeton: Princeton University Press, 1983), p.109.
20. Morison, op.cit., p.379
21. Babcock, Kendrick, *The Rise of American Nationality 1811-1819* (New York: Harper & Brothers, 1906), p.68
22. Commanger, Hemry Steele, *Documents of American History* vol.I (Englewood Cliffs: Prentice-Hall, 1973) pp.207-209.
23. Rutland, Robert Allen, *The Presidency of James Madison* (Lawrence: University of Kansas Press, 1990), pp.100-104.
24. Babcock, op.cit., pp.168-186.
25. Hickey, op.cit., pp.302-303.
26. Ibid., p.46.

CHAPTER III THE SPANISH-AMERICAN WAR

1. Chidsey, Donald Barr, *The Spanish-American War* (New York: Crown Publishers, 1971), pp.12-14.
2. Marrin, Albert, *The Spanish-American War* (New York: Atheneum, 1991), pp.16-17.
3. Chidsey, op.cit., pp.53-57.

SOURCES AND BIBLIOGRAPHIC NOTES

4. Rickover, Hyman G., *How the Battleship* Maine *Was Destroyed* (Washington, D.C.: Government Printing Office, 1976).
5. Beard, Charles A. and Mary R., *The Rise of American Civilization,* vol. II, (New York: Macmillan, 1939), p.370.
6. Morison, Samuel Eliot, *The Oxford History of the American People* (New York: Oxford University Press, 1965), pp.800-801.
7. Chidsey, op.cit., p.44.
8. Keller, Alan, *The Spanish-American War: A Compact History* (New York: Hawthorn Books, 1969), p.13.
9. Muzzey, David Saville, *An American History* (Boston: Ginn & Co., 1911), p.576.
10. Marrin, op.cit., p.31.
11. Dierks, Jack Cameron, *A Leap to Arms* (Philadelphia: Lippincott, 1970), p.24.
12. Muzzey, op.cit., p.569.
13. Beer, Thomas, *Hannah, Crane, and the Mauve Decade* (New York: Knopf, 1941), p.529.
14. Morris, Edmund, *The Rise of Theodore Roosevelt* (New York: Coward, McCann & Geoghegan, 1979).
15. Morris, Ibid., pp.259-260.
16. Morris, Ibid., p.566.
17. Keller, op.cit., pp.40-41.
18. Miller, Nathan, *Theodore Roosevelt: A Life* (New York: William Morrow and Co., 1992), p.271.
19. Marrin, op.cit., p.23.
20. Rhodes, James Ford, *The McKinley and Roosevelt Administrations* (New York: Macmillan, 1923), p.64.
21. Millis, Walter, *The Martial Spirit* (Cambridge: The Riverside Press, 1981), p.138.
22. Morrison, op.cit., p.801.
23. Commanger, Henry Steele, *Documents of American History*, vol.II (Englewood Cliffs: Prentice-Hall, 1973), p.1.
24. Keller, op.cit., pp.42-43.

25. Beard, op.cit., Vol.II, p.482.
26. Chidsey, op.cit., p.70.

CHAPTER IV   THE VIETNAM WAR
1. *Department of State Bulletin*, Washington, DC,
   August 24, 1964.
2. An excellent history of Vietnam can be found in
   Karnow, Stanley, *Vietnam: A History*, (New York: Penguin
   Books, 1984).
   A more concise summary is included in the opening
   chapters of
   Kahin, George McTurnan and Lewis, John Wilson, *The
   United States in Vietnam* (New York: Dial Press, 1967).
   A different view, emphasizing political and economic
   forces, can be found in:
   Kolko, Gabriel, *Anatomy of a War* (New York: Pantheon
   Books, 1983).
   This section used these and other sources.
3. Karnow, op.cit.,p.163.
4. Karnow, Ibid., p.194.
5. Kahin and Lewis, op.cit., p.33.
6. Kahin and Lewis, Ibid., p.32.
7. Karnow, op.cit., pp.212-214.
8. Kahin and Lewis, op.cit., p.53
9. Lacouture, Jean, *Vietnam: Between Two Truces* (New
   York: Vintage Books, 1966), p.63.
10. *Public Papers of the Presidents of the United States:
    John F. Kennedy, 1961*, (Washington, D.C.: Government
    Printing Office, 1962), pp.305-306.
11. *United States – Vietnam Relations, 1945-1967*, Book 2,
    Part B (Washington: Department of Defense, 1971),
    pp.53-57
12. *Public Papers of the Presidents of the United States:
    Dwight D. Eisenhower, 1954* (Washington, D.C.: Govern
    ment Printing Office, 1958), pp.381-390.
13. Karnow, op.cit., pp.268-270.

14. Kolko, op.cit., p.113.
15. Karnow, op.cit., p.342.
16. Kolko, op.cit., p.113.
17. LaFeber, Walter, Introduction to Part IV of *America in Vietnam: A Documentary History* (Garden City, NY: Anchor Books, 1985), p.231.
18. Karnow, op.cit., pp.382-392.
19. *Department of State Bulletin*, August 24, 1964, Washington, DC.
20. LaFeber, op.cit., p.232
21. *The New York Times*, November 30, 1992, p.1.
22. Shawcross, William, *Side-Show* (New York: Simon & Schuster, 1979).

CHAPTER V THE AMERICAN REVOLUTION

1. Commager, Henry Steele, *Documents of American History*, vol.I, "First Charter of Virginia" (Englewood Cliffs, NJ: Prentice-Hall, 1973), p.10.
2. Trevelyan, George Otto, *The American Revolution*, Richard B. Morris, ed. (New York: David McKay Co., 1964), p.2.
3. Trevalyan, op.cit., p.86.
4. Commanger, op.cit.,"The Intolerable Acts," pp.71-74.
5. Commanger, op.cit,. "Galloway's Plan of Union," pp.81-82.
6. Hacker, Louis M., *The Triumph of American Capitalism* (New York: Simon & Schuster, 1940), pp.145-170.
7. Andrews, Charles M., *The Colonial Period of American History*, vol.IV (New Haven: Yale University Press, 1938).
8. There are a number of scholarly biographies of Samuel Adams, including
    Wells, William Vincent, *The Life and Public Services of Samuel Adams*, 3 volumes, (Boston: Little, Brown, and Company, 1865)

Harlow, Ralph Volney, *Samuel Adams, Promoter of the American Revolution* (New York: Henry Holt & Company, 1923).

Beach, Stewart, *Samuel Adams: The Fateful Years, 1764-1776* (New York: Dodd, Mead & Company, 1965).

A more recent biography in the popular vein is:

Chidsey, Donald Barr, *The World of Samuel Adams* (Nashville: Thomas Nelson, 1974).

9. Muzzey, David Saville, *An American History* (Boston: Ginn & Company, 1917), p.107.

10. Commanger, Henry Steele, and Morris, Richard, *The Spirit of Seventy-Six* (New York: Harber & Row, 1958), p.271.

11. Nevins,Alan and Commanger, Henry Steele, *A Short History of the United States*, (New York: Alfred A. Knopf, 1968), p.106.

12. Nevins and Commanger, op.cit., pp.105-107.

13. For further information on Canada's history and government, the reader may wish to consult the following:

Brebner, J. Bartlett, *Canada: A Modern History* (Ann Arbor: University of Michigan Press, 1970)

Careless, J.M.S., *Canada: A Story of Challenge* (Toronto: The Macmillan Company of Canada, 1970)

Duggan, William Redman, *Our Neighbors Upstairs: The Canadians* (Chicago: Nelson-Hall, 1979)

Lower, Arthur, *Colony to Nation: A History of Canada*, (Toronto: Longmans, Green, 1946)

14. Some sources on Australian history and government include the following:

Hughes, Robert, *The Fatal Shore* (New York: Alfred A. Knopf, 1987)

Sawer, Geoffrey, *Seventy-five Years of Australian Federalism* (Melbourne: University of Melbourne Press, 1977)

15. Some sources on New Zealand history and govern
ment are:

Sinclair, Keith, *A History of New Zealand* (New York: Penguin USA, 1986)

Hawke, Gary, *The Making of New Zealand: An Economic History* (Cambridge, Eng.: Cambridge Press, 1985)

Oliver, W.H., *The Oxford History of New Zealand*, (Oxford: Oxford University Press, 1981)

CHAPTER VI   THE CIVIL WAR

1. Sources consulted for this section on slavery and politics include

Stampp, Kenneth M., *The Peculiar Institution*, (New York: Alfred A. Knopf, 1956)

Catton, Bruce, *The Coming Fury* (Garden City: Doubleday & Co., 1961)

Nevins, Allen, and Commanger, Henry Steele, *A Short History of the United States* (New York: Alfred A. Knopf, 1968)

Beard, Charles A. and Mary R., *The Rise of American Civilization*, (New York: Macmillan, 1939)

Morrison, Samuel Eliot, *The Oxford History of the American People* (New York: Oxford University Press, 1965)

Muzzey, David Saville, *An American History* (Boston: Ginn & Co., 1911)

2. Commanger, Henry Steele, *Documents of American History*, vol.I, "The Northwest Ordinance" (Englewood Cliffs: Prentice-Hall, 1973), p.132.

3. Ibid., "The Missouri Compromise", pp.224-226.

4. Ibid., "The Fugitive Slave Act", p.322

5. Coit, Margaret, *John C. Calhoun: American Portrait* (Boston: Houghton Mifflin Company, 1950), pp.492-494.

6. Rhodes, James Ford, *Lectures on the American Civil War* (New York: Macmillan, 1913), pp.2-16.
7. Benson, Lee, *Toward a Scientific Study of History* (Philadelphia: J.B. Lippincott Co., 1972), p.323.
8. Nevins, Allen, *The Emergence of Lincoln*, (New York: Charles Scribner's Sons, 1950), p.37.
9. Muzzey, op.cit., p.410.
10. Commanger, op.cit., "South Carolina Ordinance of Secession," p.372.
11. Ibid.,"The Constitution of the Confederate States of America", pp.376-384.
12. Ibid., "Lincoln's First Inaugaral Address", p.385.
13. Catton, op.cit., pp.271-325.
14. Beard, op.cit., vol. II, chap. XVII and XVIII.
15. Ramsdell, Charles W., "The Natural Limits of Slavery Expansion," *Mississippi Valley Historical Review*, Vol. 16 (1929), pp.151-171.
16. Randall, James G, *Lincoln the Liberal Statesman* (New York: Dodd, Mead & Co., 1940).
17. Muzzey, *op.cit.*, p.486.
18. Ibid., p.423.
19. Sandburg, Carl, *Abraham Lincoln: The Prairie Years and the War Years* (New York: Harcourt, Brace, 1954), p.227.
18. Wilson, Paul, "The End of the Velvet Revolution," *The New York Review of Books* (August 13, 1992), p.64.
19. The description of events in the U.S.S.R in 1990-1991 is based on news items in *The New York Times*, particularly the issues of January 3 and 4, July 18, August 19 and 24, September 6, and December 22, 1991.

CHAPTER VII   THE FIRST WORLD WAR
1. Aronson, Theo, *Crowns in Conflict* (Manchester, NH: Salem House Publishers, 1986), pp.80-81. This book

focuses on the European monarchs and their families during the period of 1910 - 1918.

2. Constant, Stephen, *Foxy Ferdinand, Tsar of Bulgaria* (London: Sidgwick and Jackson, 1979), p.288.

3. Tuchman, Barbara W., *The Guns of August* (New York: The Macmillan Company, 1962), pp.17-18. Although most of this book is concerned with the initial maneuvers and battles of the war, the introductory chapters are a good summary of the prewar situation in each of the great powers.

4, Barnes, Harry Elmer, The Genesis of the World War, (New York: Alfred A. Knopf, Inc., 1927), pp.654-662.

5. Morton, Frederic. *Thunder at Twilight* (New York: Charles Scribner's Sons, 1989), pp. 92-03. This book is a well-written and well-documented account of the events in Vienna leading up to and follwing the assassination of Archduke Ferdinand.

6. Hale, Oron J., *The Great Illusion 1900 - 1914* (New York, Harper & Row, 1971), pp. 292-295. This book includes interesting chapters on the social, cultural, and political history in the period just before the war.

7. Morton, op.cit., pp.282-304.

8. Hale, op.cit., pp.308-312.

9. Stokesbury, James L., *A Short History of World War I* (New York: William Morrow and Co., 1981), pp.216-222.

10. Muzzy, David Saville, *An American History* (Boston: Ginn & Company, 1917), p.xxiv.

11. Kennedy, Paul, *The Rise and Fall of the Great Powers* (New York: Random House, 1987), p.264.

12. Baldwin, Hanson W,, *World War I: An Outline History* (New York: Harper and Row, 1962), pp.106-107.

13. Ibid., pp.156-157.

14. Stokesbury, op.cit, p.323.

UNNECESSARY WARS?

CHAPTER VIII   THE SECOND WORLD WAR
1. Baldwin, Hanson W., *The Crucial Years 1939 - 1941* (New York: Harper & Row, 1976), pp.5-8.
2. Taylor, A.J.P., *The Origins of the Second World War* (New York: Atheneum, 1983), pp.97- 100.
3. Ibid., p.186.
4. Watt, Donald Cameron, *How War Came: The Immediate Origins of the Second World War 1938 - 1939* (New York: Pantheon Books, 1989), pp.313-338.
5. Taylor, A.P., op.cit., pp.266-278.
6. Baldwin, op.cit., pp.9-11.
7. Samagalski, Alan, and Buckley, Michael, *China* (Berkely, CA: Lonely Planet Publications, 1984), pp.31 - 33.
8. Baldwin, op.cit, p.141.
9. Ibid., p.430.
10. Gilbert, Martin, *The Second World War: A Complete History* (New York: Henry Holt and Compamy, 1989), p.735.

CHAPTER IX   THE KOREAN WAR
1. Stokesbury, James L., *A Short History of the Korean War* (New York: William Morrow and Co., 1988), pp.21-23.
2. Ridgeway, Matthew B., *The Korean War* (Garden City, NY: Doubleday & Co., 1967), p.7.
3. Hastings, Max, *The Korean War* (New York: Simon and Schuster, 1987), p.27.
4. Cumings, Bruce, *The Origins of the Korean War* (Princeton: Princeton University Press, 1981), pp.188-190.
5. Whelan, Richard, *Drawing the Line: The Korean War, 1950-1953* (Boston: Little, Brown, and Company, 1990), pp.44-47.
6. Hastings, op.cit., p.42-43.
7. Ridgeway, op.cit., p.14.
8. Hastings, op.cit., pp.56-57.

9. Stokesbury, op.cit., pp.36-37.

10. Ibid., pp.253-254.

CHAPTER X THREE POTENTIAL WARS THAT WERE
AVOIDED

1. Richardson, James D. ed., *Messages and Papers of the Presidents*, vol.IV (New York: Bureau of National Literature), Vol.IV, p.379.

2. Muzzey, James Saville, *An American History* (Boston: Ginn & Company, 1911), p.342.

3. Additional information on the Oregon controversy can be found in
  Bergeron, Paul H. *The Presidency of James K. Polk* (Lawrence: University of Kansas Press, 1987).
  McCormac, Eugene Irvin, *James K. Polk: A Political Biography* (New York: Russell & Russell, 1965).

4. Richardson, op.cit., Vol. IX, p.655

5. Commanger, Henry Steele, ed., *Documents of American History*, vol.I (Englewoood Cliffs, NJ: Prentice-Hall, Inc., 1973), p.620.

6. Miller, Nathan, *Theodore Roosevelt: A Life* (New York: William Morrow and Company, 1992), p.235.

7. Additional information on the Venezuelan boundary controversy can be found in
  Nevins, Allan, *Grover Cleveland* (New York: Dodd, Mead & Co, 1930).
  Koehler, Charles, *The Monroe Doctrine: A Complete History* (New York: J.J. Little & Ives Co., 1925).

8. A detailed accoubnt of the events summarized in the preceeding paragraphs can be found in
  Matthews, Herbert L., *Revolution in Cuba* (New York: Charles Scribner's Sons, 1975).

9. Since 1987, there have been five conferences on the Cuban Missile Crisis, which have substantially altered and augmented initial accounts. The fifth, held in Cuba in January 1992, was reported by one of the

participants, Arthur Schlesinger, Jr. in
"Four Days with Fidel: A Havana Diary," *New York Review of Books*, vol.39, issue 6, (March 26, 1992), pp.22-29. The statement on the Soviet tactical missiles was made by General Anatoly Gribikov during that conference.
10. Kennedy, Robert F., *Thirteen Days* (New York: W.W. Norton & Company, 1969), pp.24-28.
11. Tapes of the ExComm meetings have recently been declassified. A summary of the tapes is available in an article by Brian Dooley:
"The Cuban Missile Crisis — 30 Years On," *History Today*, Vol.42, (October 1992), pp.6-8.
12. Sorenson, Theodore C., *Kennedy* (New York: Harper & Row, 1965), pp.676-689.
13. Brugioni, Dino, *Eyeball to Eyeball: The Inside Story of the Cuban Missile Crisis* (New York: Random House, 1990), pp.356-360.
14. Sorenson, op.cit., p.703-704.
15. Brugioni, op.cit., p.484
16. Kennedy, op.cit., p.119.

CHAPTER XI   PATIENCE AND FORTITUDE

1. Draper, Theodore, "Presidential Wars," *The New York Review of Books*, (September 26, 1991), pp.64-74.
2. Forsberg, Randall, "Creating a Cooperative Security System", *Boston Review*, (November/December 1992).
3. Forsberg, Randall, "Defense Cuts and Cooperative Security in the Post-Cold War World", *Boston Review*, (May/July 1992).
3. Laurenti, Jeff, *Partners for Peace* (New York: United Nations Association of the U.S.A., 1992).
4. Woito, Robert, *To End War: A New Approach to Inter national Conflict* (New York: Pilgrim Press, 1982).

INDEX

INDEX

INDEX

INDEX

INDEX